Letters of William Still

Letters of William Still

With an introductory biographical sketch

THE BANNER OF TRUTH TRUST

THE BANNER OF TRUTH TRUST
3 Murrayfield Road, Edinburgh EH12 6EL
P.O. Box 621, Carlisle, Pennsylvania 17013, U.S.A.

This selection first published by The Banner of Truth Trust 1984

ISBN 0 85151 378 6

Phototypeset in 11/12 Garamond by
Nuprint Services Ltd., Harpenden, Herts.
Reproduced, printed and bound in Great Britain by
Hazell Watson & Viney Limited,
Member of the BPCC Group,
Aylesbury, Bucks

CONTENTS

BIOGRAPHICAL INTRODUCTION

It is unlikely that the name of William Still will feature prominently in the official annals of the Church of Scotland. He has never been Moderator of its General Assembly, or convener of any of its major committees. He has not often featured in the religious media. In fact, almost all of his life has been lived in the city of Aberdeen, somewhat 'off the beaten track', even in days of North Sea oil. Yet it is doubtful whether any other individual in his Church during this time has had such a profound and widespread influence. Certainly no Professor in the Divinity Colleges could claim the love and loyalty of his former students to the extent that scores of ministers would look to William Still as their friend and counsellor. Some of them would openly confess that they learned far more about the work of the Christian ministry from him than they did from their theological teachers. In many ways, of course, that is how it always should be. But in William Still's case it is true to a very remarkable degree.

The fact that so many ministers in the Church of Scotland exercise preaching ministries in which the Scriptures are systematically expounded is largely, if not entirely, the result of William Still's example and experience. Systematic, expository teaching, in which a book of the Bible is expounded, section by section, has never been a leading feature of the Scottish pulpit. But, as in the days of the Church Fathers, and the Continental Reformers, when there has been a famine of the Word of God in the land, there is no better way for its truth to be relearned. This 'method' of preaching has come to be used by so many evangelical ministers in the Church of Scotland today that it is one of the most noticeable features in the changing face of the Kirk. And this is a change which has taken place within the lifetime and long ministry of William Still, minister of Gilcomston South Church, Aberdeen since 1945.

During Mr Still's ministry letter writing has been a major part of his work. Each week he engages in correspondence with ministers, missionaries, Christian leaders, students and former members, spread throughout the world; many people, known and unknown to him, write regularly for counsel and advice. And once each month the *Gilcomston South Congregational Record* carries a pastoral letter which is written particularly for this wider readership. At first intended exclusively for the congregation, the magazine (which also contains Bible study notes for each month) now has a circulation of around one thousand copies. The pastoral letter has consequently taken on the character of an 'encyclical' which gives not only pastoral counsel, but speaks to the issues of the day, and documents the work of God in the congregation and throughout the world-wide church of Christ. These letters were all written with a wider readership in mind, and it is from more than four hundred of them, written during thirty-seven years of William Still's ministry, that this compilation has been made. Even this small selection helps to show why his ministry, undoubtedly unique, sometimes regarded as eccentric by critical observers, has had such a widespread influence.

Pathway to the Ministry

William Still was born in Aberdeen on the 8th of May 1911. His parents, William and Helen Still, were both from the little fishing village of Gardenstown, some fifty miles north of Aberdeen along the coast. Seven children were born to them, five boys and two girls. One child (called William) survived only nine months; but his name was preserved in the family.

From his earliest childhood young William was taken to the meetings of the Salvation Army Corps in Aberdeen. Already by the age of thirteen he was a decided Christian. But it was not until another twenty years had passed that this early discipleship came to its full flowering when in 1945 he was called to his first (and, as it has proved to be, his only) pastoral change, the congregation of Gilcomston South Church, Aberdeen. He has briefly summarised that first half of his life in these words:

> From the age of seven I suffered a series of set-backs in health which seemed by adolescence to confirm my inability to make anything of my life. I tried to work with my father in the fish trade at fourteen, turned to music at seventeen, to Christian service in the Salvation Army[1] at twenty-three, and in six months was in a state of nervous exhaustion. Four years later, somewhat improved in health, I offered for Salvation Army work again, but was rejected on the grounds of health, and immediately decided that I must try to fulfil my, by then, clear call to divine service, elsewhere than in that branch of the Christian Church.[2]

Clearly these events were a major part of the remarkable providence of God in his life. Had he remained in the Salvation Army, or indeed become an officer in its ranks, it seems certain that his ministry could never have developed in the way it eventually did.

[1] Letter 27 recalls some of the lasting influence of two Salvation Army officers on his life and ministry.

[2] *The History of Gilcomston South Church, I p.*35.

Now in his late twenties, he studied for entrance to the University of Aberdeen (having left school at the age of thirteen), and during the Second World War he prepared at Christ's College, Aberdeen, for the ministry of the Church of Scotland.

On completing his course of study he spent a year in Glasgow as assistant to Dr William Fitch, minister of Springburn Hill Church (and later of the historic Knox Presbyterian Church, Toronto). During this period he was involved in a train accident which set in motion a series of incidental events which were to prove, in the providence of God, to be highly significant for his future work. His life was spared—he suffered only a broken ankle. Three months of hospitalisation were followed by a period of recuperation in Aberdeen.

In fact an approach had already been made to him by Gilcomston South Church, to explore the possibility of him becoming their new minister. But he had followed the advice given to him by one of his College Professors never to accept a call to his home town (advice which, at the time, may have sounded double-edged!). He declined, politely but firmly. However, his hospitalisation, and now his return to Aberdeen for recuperation led to a surprising outcome. He has recalled the events which followed:

> It was while hirpling around Aberdeen, first on two crutches, then on one, and on two sticks, then on one, that my maternal aunt Bella, recently widowed, came to the West Church of St. Andrew with me one evening for the 7 o'clock service. It was an informal service and the minister chatted with people in the aisles afterwards. He saw me and asked what I was going to do. I said, 'Erskine Blackburn of Holburn Central Church (who was interim moderator in the vacancy) has asked if I will accept a call

to Gilcomston South. What do you think?' He said, 'I wouldn't. My assistant says, "Not even Saint Paul could do anything with that place"...'

Later that evening while waiting at the bus stop, my aunt asked me, 'What was the minister saying?' I told her. 'And what do you think of that?' she asked. Then, almost casually and with, as I recall it, a far-away tone in my voice and no sense of the dramatic, and certainly no sense of destiny, I replied, 'Maybe less than Paul will do'.[3]

The call was later accepted. The West Church assistant minister was not merely being cynical in his remarks about the condition of the Gilcomston congregation whose building stood almost directly across Union Street from the West Church itself. The fact that William Still's 'call' to be minister was signed by 74 members and 2 adherents provides ample testimony to that. For there were almost 600 names on the congregational roll. Earlier, during the vacancy, between December 1943 and June 1945, discussions had taken place about the possibility of merging the congregation with another. Fewer than seventy members had attended those meetings. Only 58 were present at the meeting at which it was decided to continue as a separate congregation. Of that number, 18 voted for union with another congregation, 14 for dissolving, and only 26 for continuing. Only 5% of the congregational roll, therefore, voted to continue. Even assuming that many members were engaged in war duties, these statistics were far from encouraging to a new minister! But William Still was deeply conscious that the hand of God was ordering his path, and as he often remarked in later years, it was this consciousness which carried him through many discouragements, frustrations and times of disappointment.

[3] *Ibid.*, p.36.

Four Decades of Service

The ministry at Gilcomston South from 1945 onwards has been notable for many reasons. Its length (now 38 years) is obviously one of them, although by no means the most important. In fact this one ministry has, in some respects, been several ministries. During these four decades the membership of the congregation has changed several times, only a small nucleus having been present throughout its entire life. Further, the emphases in the ministry have also changed, perhaps two or three times, according to the needs of the congregation, the spheres of service into which it has been led, and the specific burdens in ministry and prayer which it has experienced:

> No man and congregation can go on year after year doing the same things and keep alive unless there is not only change but sequence, rhythm, and (we hope) progress towards solid spiritual achievement, that not only meets the needs of our day, but points forward, prophetically, to the spiritual needs of tomorrow and to a new generation.[4]

The first months of ministry, in the immediate aftermath of the War years, were marked by a blaze of evangelistic activity. In particular this followed a remarkable visit to Aberdeen by the young American evangelist, Billy Graham, then with the Youth For Christ organisation. Two meetings were held in Gilcomston South in 1946. Mr Still recalls:

> The first evening I took the opening prayer, and moved to see the packed congregation, enjoyed liberty in speaking to God. When I returned to my seat in the choir pew, I found myself seated next to Billy. In his expansive human way he turned and put his arm round me and

[4] Letter of June 1970, (p. 109).

whispered, 'Will you come to America?' 'Just like that?' I asked. 'Yes,' he said...[5]

But William Still did not go to America (either then, or later). Instead he threw his energies into a series of Saturday-night gatherings for young people, held in his own church. These evangelistic rallies had everything—choir, organ, piano, solos, testimonies, addresses! Multitudes of young people crowded the building and many of them professed to become Christians, large numbers of military cadets among them. Converts 'were falling into the Lord's lap like plums', he later wrote. Suddenly, and very dramatically indeed, Gilcomston South seemed to have been resurrected from the dead. Financially too it prospered, and within a couple of years givings quadrupled. From many points of view the ministry seemed to be successful and prospering. It had not been true, after all, that 'not even Saint Paul could do anything' with Gilcomston South. A lesser than Paul had been used of God!

Yet, at the same time, something was happening in William Still's own heart and spirit which was to redirect his ministry in a way, and with repercussions, which neither he nor others could have anticipated.

The Saturday evening rallies were intended as evangelistic occasions. Because the Gilcomston South Sunday evening service began after that of most other congregations in town, large numbers attended that service in addition to their own. But now, on Sundays, the preacher was beginning to find a new depth and penetration, as well as a new satisfaction, in teaching the Bible. Almost by accident, or so it seemed at the time, he began to preach consecutively through passages of Scripture, and soon, whole books. He did not know then that he had rediscovered the mode of

[5] *The History of Gilcomston South Church*, I p.42.

preaching which had been so signally used by some of the great Fathers of the early church, and by the Reformers Luther and Calvin. But he did recognize an authority and solidity in this ministry which made the other service seem superficial. He now saw that the task to which God was calling him was to build strong Christian character through the ministry of God's Word, patiently expounded and searchingly applied to the consciences of his hearers.

William Still decided to put these convictions to the test. He abandoned the Saturday night rallies and began a prayer meeting instead. The effect was both instantaneous and dramatic, at least in numerical terms. Between one Sunday and the next numbers attending the Sunday evening service dropped by between *two and three hundred*. Some accused him of driving young Christians into the cinemas on Saturday nights, because there was nowhere else for them to go! The answer (which he usually refrained from giving) was all too obvious to him. There was no need to go to the cinema; let them come to the meeting for prayer! What better way to spend the evening? There can be little doubt that the experience left an indelible conviction in his mind and on his ministry. Real Christianity, with its foundations in the basic elements of biblical teaching, demands real consecration. It demands reality most of all. And that, he had come to see very painfully, was ground on which many professing Christians were all too reluctant to stand. From that time on his ministry was almost invariably to small, rather than larger congregations, to a few hundred, rather than to the many hundreds of the early days. It would probably be true to say that, almost from the beginning of his work, his ministry was on lines quite distinct from the general trends among evangelicals.

What had come home to him with almost prophetic clarity and simplicity was that the work of the pastor is to feed and tend the flock of God. He now consecrated his time and energies with fresh vigour to fulfilling this calling. Indeed, he was sufficiently assured of the summons God had given him to share his personal commitment with his people in the Congregational Letter for January 1948:

> I have cut out every external activity and interest, and every moment of my time is solely devoted to the work of Gilcomston and the needs of its wider congregation (apart from such engagements beyond the bounds of the city as are approved). There is no part of me, or of my life, that I will withhold from the work that God has called me to, and I am determined that no mere form or convention will hinder me from giving the message in the church in a way that will be understood even by the most unlettered person.

That commitment to his own people has sometimes reached great lengths. In 1974 he refused the increasingly rare honour of the award of Doctor of Divinity from the University of Aberdeen. When asked once why he had done so, he simply replied that he did not want to give his people the embarrassment of thinking that they should have to call him 'Doctor' after so many years of calling him 'Mister'. Doubtless there was more to the refusal than that; but he was resolved that nothing should divert him from, or be an impediment to his great task. Throughout the years this commitment has remained and determined the pattern of his life. Although a bachelor, and therefore more free to accept invitations away from home, he has sought increasingly to conserve his energies for the work to which he has been called in Aberdeen. He has seen that such a ministry, exercised faithfully and in the power of the Spirit, can reach to the ends of the earth. Thus Gilcomston has been his life. 'There is', he has often been heard to say, 'more than enough to do at home'. For him that is underlined by the fact that, although he has preached and commented[6] on the whole Bible at least three times, there is always fresh light breaking out to him from the Word of God.

It would be impossible in this brief introduction even to begin to sketch out the pattern of events in the years of ministry which lie behind these letters. Happily, despite his busy life, Mr Still has recorded his own impressions in his *History of Gilcomston South Church,*[7] and readers are directed to those volumes for further information. But some comment needs to be made about the general life of the congregation in order to set the scene for reading the Congregational Letters.

Congregational Life

Gilcomston South Church today has around 400 members. Set, as it is, in Union Street, Aberdeen's main thoroughfare, it is ideally situated to draw members from all parts of the city, and students from the University, Divinity College and other Colleges in the city. Today, many more members and past members or adherents are serving the Lord elsewhere, than the number of members on the roll. These, along with others, constitute the readership of the Congregational Letter. This helps to explain why it has grown from its early status as a pastoral letter to the congregation, to a letter which deals with a wide range of topics.

In the congregation itself, a main burden of the ministry had been to seek to apply biblical principles to the entire life of the church. One of the themes which recurs in the letters is that of 'unstarching the church'—breaking away from

[6] The Congregational Record contains a commentary on daily Bible reading passages, as well as a Letter.

[7] In 2 volumes, available from Gilcomston South Church, Union Street, Aberdeen.

unbiblical traditions in order to create an atmosphere of fellowship. So seriously has this been taken that a number of years ago the pews in the downstairs section of the church building were removed, the floor completely carpeted, and moveable seating introduced in order to facilitate after-church fellowship. News of this spread to churches in which the removal of pews would be almost akin to a denial of the faith, so that the question, 'Have you heard that Willie Still has removed all the pews in his church?' was not only slightly inaccurate, but conveyed the impression of a minister who had gone on the rampage!

Almost four decades of ministry in a single congregation set in a University city is an exceedingly rare occurrence. Mr Still has had the opportunity of observing the work of God in one place with a long-term perspective. He is therefore conscious that other ministers and congregations may share the benefits of such a long experience. This is the main reason for the frequent references in the letters to what he has seen in Gilcomston South. Some few comments on the pattern of church life there will guide the reader through the letters which address themselves to the subject of church fellowship.

The basic conclusion which Mr Still has reached about the life of the church is that it should be simply structured—so simply, indeed, that it could be transported to any place, time and circumstances and continue to operate:

> What we are trying to do is to build a church which in all essentials belongs to the ages and incorporates all the biblical elements which alone can stand the test of time, and yet which leaves people wonderfully free within that simple all-embracing scheme to adopt, improvise and modify the pattern as may be expedient for this time and

that place and these people, here or there, whether in the highlands or lowlands.

For this reason there are no organizations in the congregation, with the minor exception of a Sunday School for children under seven. Beyond that the church is seen as a family, and its gatherings are regarded as relevant to all the members. This applies equally to the two Sunday services, the mid-week Bible Study and the Saturday night meeting for prayer. The central emphasis is on the ministry of the Word and prayer, worship and fellowship, and the consequent witness of the church as individuals and as a fellowship in the city and beyond. Some of the struggles to establish this simple pattern, in a denomination largely unused to it, are recorded in the following pages.

The letters in this selection have been chosen for their inherent value, but also to provide a chronicle of a faithful ministry. In them, some of William Still's chief convictions clearly emerge: theological convictions about the authority of Scripture, the Person of Christ, the nature of the gospel; important ecclesiastical insights and pastoral convictions on the subject of loving, human care for God's people.

Perhaps this last conviction most distinguishes William Still in the eyes of his friends. For many of them the greatest compliment they could pay to him would be to say that his ministry has reflected what he himself has written of the ministry of Jesus Christ: 'He always had time for individuals in need, and always made them feel that they were worthy of his closest attention'.[8] It is this measure of genuine pastoral care which gives the ring of authenticity to many of the things he says in the pages which follow.

SINCLAIR B. FERGUSON
Edinburgh 1983

[8] Letter of January, 1972 (p. 125).

1/NEW BEGINNINGS

September 1946

My Dear Friends,

Since I came to Gilcomston I have been most anxious to reach you all with the Gospel message. This I have not been able to do, for many members (I am not prepared to say what proportion), do not come to Church. Therefore, if many of you will not come to Church, then the Church must come to you. This means I must visit you, and I confess I have not got on very well with this part of my work, partly because of the needs of the sick, and partly because of the needs of the innumerable multitude of people of all congregations and none, who come to me in all manner of troubles. True, my own congregation must come first, but no man can refuse to help anyone who comes in great and urgent need.

Frankly, much of my time is taken up with this work. The only other way that the Church can come to you is by means of a periodic record and message, and I am anxious that such a message should reach every home in our congregation each month. The preparation of this will take some work, but it is necessary, both to record our activities and to send a message alike to those who cannot and to those who will not come to Church. The plain truth is that many have slipped into membership far too easily. It has meant little to them and has cost them little. They therefore value it scarcely at all. I still find a few who do not know what is going on at Gilcomston, although the news is widespread.

Simple and direct Gospel messages are given, and a call is made, not only for attendance and thought, but for action. Many are unprepared for this. I am tempted to say that I regret if the smooth, easy flow of Church of Scotland congregational life has been disturbed, but the truth is that it is not I who has changed the Church, but God. All those who attend must know that whether we like it or not, God has put His hand upon Gilcomston and said, '*I want this place for my work*'.

God's work is to save men and women out of the world to be witnesses for Him. The Church today is so worldly and dead that it does not like this, and does not agree with it. But, my friends, before God I say it does not matter what we think or what we like. What God says is true, and we must face it, and if we do not face it here, we shall have to face it hereafter. We may sit down and mope because the sky is not pink. We may even put on rose-coloured spectacles, but the sky when you can see it, is blue, and that is a fact. Similarly, we all have to face death. We may not like to think about death. We may say that we do not know what happens after death. But that is not true, for the Bible, especially the New Testament, is full of revelations about happenings after death, both for those who are saved and for those who are not.

My dear friends, you may take up one of several attitudes. You may decide to change your congregation, or, (which shows a manifest lack of character), you may decide to continue letting things drift; but while you remain a member of Gilcomston and I am the minister, then you must be reminded, as often as I have the opportunity, that you are not your own, God made you, Christ died for you, and if you do not respond to His love here, you will have to face His judgment hereafter.

Let me say also that while you may have heard of the

thunderous and terrifying preaching in Gilcomston, I am sure you will find that behind it there is a fellowship of love, harmony, sweetness, and kindness such as I myself have never found anywhere else. The plain truth is that God the Holy Spirit is with us, helping us in all manner of ways, and we give thanks to God that not only before the congregation in public, but in the courts of the Church, and in all private and confidential business, there is a complete absence of bitterness and ill-will, or even of criticism, and I marvel that in the transformation which has taken place in the life and work of the congregation there has been such good-will and forbearance. Even where members, and even perhaps office-bearers, have not agreed with, or liked, the line that has been taken, there has been on the whole a spirit of real Christian charity and patience, and this has made the task all the easier.

Let us give glory to our God for all He has done and all He is doing in our midst. I pray that our own membership, especially in the outer circle and on the fringe, may more and more enter into warm and healthy fellowship with us, and may find the satisfaction which comes from knowing and serving Christ our Saviour and Lord.

Yours warmly and sincerely in the Master's service.

WILLIAM STILL

P.S. I should say that I am very conscious of many faults and failings, and it is in the interest of the Church and congregation that I should be told about them. If I have done anything that I ought not to have done, or have left anything undone that I ought to have done, please tell me, and I think you will find me ready to confess and to make amends. Do not hesitate to speak frankly to me about all things, for I do not take offence.

2/SIGNS OF EARLY FRUIT

November 1946

My Dear Friends,

Now that all the special meetings are over, and I have returned from the campaign at Troon, I feel the strong necessity for us all to settle down to our own work. I know that some feel that I respond to too many outside calls, but I assure you that I have only responded to a fraction of them, and there are those, not only in Aberdeen, but in the main centres in the South, who assure me that in these days I have a wider responsibility in the country. I fully realize this, and I praise God for every opportunity to share in His work in other centres. Yet each time I see the work in other places I am the more convinced that our greatest opportunity for doing God's work lies, not only in Aberdeen, but in Gilcomston, and I want to assure you all that, although it pains me very much not to be able to help my brother ministers, I am determined to keep my nose to the home grindstone.

There is much to be done here. There are still many 'far ben' in our congregational life who are facing the demands of the Gospel in their own hearts. I want you to know that I pray for you individually, and not as a superior person (for I am not better than any of you) but as a brother who desires you all to come to the living knowledge of our Lord. I am sure that you will all do so. I am not discouraged that many take a long time to think about personal acceptance of Christ, for it is a heavy matter, and needs much thought.

I am deeply touched to know that there are those who

have quietly and gently begun the real Christian life. I know that we Scots are not demonstrative, but when we accept Christ, even as secretly as Nicodemus, a time will come when we shall want to come out into the open as he did. I think you should know that if you are seriously thinking about the challenge of the Gospel, there are many seated around you in Gilcomston who are also doing that very thing. How lovely it will be in the future when we are all drawn so close to our Lord that we shall be bound in a fellowship, united and strong, that nothing will break! I believe there is no end to what God will do among us if we will all be humble enough to yield to Him.

One thing more! I have a feeling that some of our members would like to come along on Wednesday evenings[1], but hold back lest it give a sign that they are really interested in the spiritual life. I do want you to know that to embark on the life of the Spirit does not, and must not involve you in restricting your life to any set pattern. No one, neither the Minister, nor any other, has a right to dictate, or even to hint, at how you should run your life. St. Augustine, you know, had a motto—'Love God and do as you like'. This is a very sound maxim, and fully Scriptural. But it is the second part that attracts us. If we really love God, we shall do what He likes us to do.

Now, to close, a hint on daily Bible meditation. You cannot go wrong in the Psalms, and in John's Gospel. As you acquire a taste for Bible reading, you will want to explore other books of Scripture, but the experience of most people is that a grounding in the wonderful faith of the psalmists, and in the revelation of John in his Gospel, is a sure foundation for the Christian life. In this connection, perhaps, the most helpful feature of the services at Gilcomston is the Bible reading, in which I seek to help you to

[1] Mid-week Bible studies were held on Wednesday evenings.

understand what is often behind the form of biblical words. And we must always remember that the Bible is no ordinary book. It is a living book, and has all the advantages of a living book. To understand it, we must have the Holy Spirit in our hearts, and as we read with sincere humility He will throw His searchlight upon the page and reveal the hidden truth that the un-Christian mind, however intelligent and eager, can never see or understand.

May God bless you all.

Yours sincerely,
WILLIAM STILL

3/AN APPEAL TO NOMINAL CHRISTIANS

March 1947

My Dear People,

There are still a number on our Roll (I speak with sympathetic understanding) who do not yet see what all the religious talk is about. To them the Church means little or nothing, and they are content, as long as there is a Minister available in time of need. I do not say this in bitterness. Indeed, however much members neglect the Church, they will find the Minister on their doorstep as soon as he learns of their need, ever eager to be of assistance to them, and to bring the grace of God to bear upon their necessity.

But you must allow me to say gently that you are missing the best in life. If you loved Jesus Christ as I and many members of Gilcomston love Him, you would be prepared almost to crawl to Church to worship Him. *And I want to say that in view of God's blessing upon Gilcomston, and of the wonderful changes that God is working in the lives of those who attend there, no member who is free and able has a shadow of an excuse for not attending regularly.*

If ordinary folk are honestly seeking spiritual help, our service could not be more homely, helpful, and reverent. But, of course, if we have those in our fellowship who honestly do not want Jesus Christ, then they must accept the consequences, for theirs is the greatest sin of all, namely, that of rejecting the Perfect One.

I can tell you that the loyal members of Gilcomston are often deeply grieved at this strain in my messages (they do not know what it costs me to speak and write like this); but I cannot rest content until every member and adherent of Gilcomston South has become a willing captive to the love of Jesus Christ. My dear friends, the Gospel message is not hard. It contains all that is sweet and lovely, and tender; it is only hard to those who will not have it.

I can promise you that Gilcomston South is well on the way to becoming a real, live, spiritual fellowship, and it is high time that some had caught up or they will be left behind, or even, sad to say, left out of it altogether.

One last word! No one need be shy of coming to Gilcomston after a long absence—there are too many strangers for you to be conspicuous. Come on now, make a start—that's the hardest battle. Once you've made a beginning I am sure you will want to continue.

That God may bless you and help you is my continual prayer.

Yours sincerely,
WILLIAM STILL

4/WORDS TO PARENTS

April 1948

My Dear Friends,

I want to say a word to parents. We are greatly blessed in our work among the young at Gilcomston. And although we have much to learn yet about training them, we have a team of workers who are serious, sincere, and absolutely loyal. There is nothing we will not do for these young folk. The question is, are they getting a real grasp of the faith? Do they know Jesus Christ as Saviour and Friend?

We think there are evidences of grace in the lives of the little folk, although we too often magnify their faults. How deep in their hearts it is, we shall know when they reach the difficult transitional years, 14–15. Christ can hold children, even through the fiercest trials of adolescence. But they need guidance. It was never so hard to be a Christian in school, at play, and among the pagan youth of our day.

Parents can help most here by keeping a careful, if unseen, watch on their children's friendships, especially from 12 years onwards. They should make a point of getting to know their special friends, and gently reproving if they think them not suitable. They must help their children to form a sense of duty, and to arrange the various duties of life in a true order.

Parents' first responsibility is to inculcate in their children a sense of absolute duty (not to say love) to Christ and His Church. However much children are sent to Church, and however much pleasure and help they get out of it, the whole may be lost if, on reaching teenage years, they are allowed to put lesser duties, and even pleasures, before Christ and the Church.

What recreations and amusements children are permitted to enjoy is a very difficult matter for parents to decide, and needs guidance from God. It is a matter, not only of *where* we allow the children to go, but *when*. The real test of whether our pleasures are *right* or *wrong* is when they happen to clash with Church. What then do we do? I have little fear for any, young or old, whatever pleasures they may allow themselves, who, when a clash occurs, put Christ and His Church first. But it is a deeper question than pleasure. It is not merely Christ versus enjoyment, but Christ versus self. When we have some special call upon our time which concerns our personal advantage, what is it that suffers? Is it our work, or our leisure evenings, or our attendance at God's house? There are only two real excuses for non-attendance at God's house: (1) our own indisposition, (2) the needs of others. There is no other that God will accept.

Think seriously about this, and pray about it. It is not a plea for loyalty to the Minister, or even to the Church, but to our Saviour Christ Himself, who can only be found in the Church, which is His body.

'Seek ye *first* the kingdom of God and his righteousness, and all *these things* shall be *added* unto you.'

Yours sincerely,

WILLIAM STILL

5/THE LIFE OF THE CHURCH

June 1948

My Dear Friends,

We have been together three years, and the present ministry is beginning to take shape. We have gone through various phases, no doubt each contributing to our knowledge and experience, but there comes a time when we must ask ourselves precisely what we are trying to do.

It is the simple truth to say that our policy has been determined by a Higher Hand. The Minister knew more about what he was *not* going to do, than what he *was* going to do, when he came. Yet looking back he can see a rhythmic progress in the ministry that was not planned by him. This is seen in the changing style of the services, especially the sermons, which reveal a sequence that can only be attributed to the guidance of the Spirit.

Where is it leading? Again it is easier to say where it is not leading. If we are to wage war for God we must be very vigilant. There are subtle dangers to be faced and dealt with. Consequently within the last eighteen months drastic steps have been taken to remove all that was merely novel and sensational. An enduring ministry must be founded upon something stable. Upon what? The Word of God! Thus it has turned out that the chief characteristic of the services, Sunday morning, afternoon, evening, Wednesday and Saturday is the Bible reading, with such comments, explanations and exposition as are necessary. In short this has become a *teaching ministry*.

Is that a good thing? How does it square with the task of evangelism? For answer I refer you to Acts 9:31. 'Then had the Church rest . . . and was built up, and going on in the fear of the Lord, and in the comfort of the Holy Ghost was *multiplied.*' That is a full answer, and the best statement of policy. Evangelism must spring from the upbuilding of the Church, and the Church can only be upbuilt by the living Word of God.

The whole emphasis of the ministry is here. Some may think too much so, and wish for more social fellowship. But are they not looking to the Church for the wrong thing? If those who wish for that showed their love for Christ by attendance at the gatherings for which the Church was founded, their argument for the other side would carry weight. Do people stay away because they have no taste for spiritual things, or have they no taste for spiritual things because they stay away?

We have a full day on Sunday, a mid-week service on Wednesday and a prayer meeting on Saturday. There is nothing exciting or outwardly attractive in that. Intentionally so, it is solid meat all the time, the sort of thing for balanced intelligent Christians. It does not provide a complete system of leisure-time occupation, nor does it offer social facilities. Why should it? If we train, educate and establish our people in true Christian living, they will learn to employ their leisure time properly, and find desirable social intercourse without the aid of the Minister. Many have found for themselves Christian friends at Gilcomston, and it is surely a very odd person who cannot find in such a mixed congregation at least one person with whom he or she has affinity.

May I say what I would like to see at Gilcomston?

I would like the Sunday morning service to be the family worship of the whole congregation—no segregation of age groups, all must learn to worship together. Sunday afternoon is obviously for the young folk, and although the teaching must be graded I want 'family' worship there also part of the time. Sunday evening is devoted to the preaching of the Gospel. If you are a Christian, you may say, 'That doesn't concern me!' But it does. That is the point of this letter. If you are being upbuilt in the faith you are bound to become concerned about others. If so, there are two things to do:

(1) Attend on Sunday evening in a prayerful spirit. (You may not think this important, but if you heard the same sermon preached where there was no spirit of prayer you might not recognize it). The congregation *makes* the preacher as much as the preacher *makes* the congregation.

(2) Invite people to the service. Surely you take part in conversations during the week that lead you to invite people to Church? Seeking the lost is a thrilling adventure. Of course you will not go out and hunt them. It is by prayer and Christian living that you influence other people, often unconsciously, speaking only when the time is ripe, or when invited to do so.

Wednesday evening is the time for Bible study. I believe that it is essential to the continuance of this ministry that the congregation get into the habit of attending the mid-week service.

Then lastly, there is Saturday evening. There is a deep connection between the prayer meeting and the Sunday services. No church can live without prayer. What changes the prayers of the saints have produced in our midst! God holds Gilcomston South responsible for a Church in which His Holy Spirit is working, even if some do not choose to have it so. May God help us all to be more faithful, and to rise to the signal honour which He has bestowed upon us.

Yours sincerely,

WILLIAM STILL

6/CHILDREN AND THE CHURCH (1)

August 1948

My Dear Friends,

This month we record the beginning of Children's Church and Primary Sunday School. Our summer season is a long and arduous one, and by June we are looking forward, like all conscientious teachers, to a respite from the strain of teaching. Yet as the summer days pass we miss more and more the children and the children's work, and look forward with eagerness to the commencement of the session. We are concerned here with the background of the work.

What is Children's Church and Primary Sunday School achieving? We can never know fully what spiritual work is being accomplished, especially with children, and we must never be too eager to find out, although deeply concerned as true shepherds of the lambs. After three sessions, however, we can surely assess a little of the influence exerted upon those children who have been regular in attendance and diligent in study. We are not trying here to assess the pleasure the children have found in the work, but the lasting effect. All we will say is that the result is encouraging and promising. This is long-term work done in faith and we must be content to labour for years sowing the seed and watering it with our prayers in hope.

But when children come to adolescent years, their training and childish Christian experience must be put to the *acid test of decision*. It is one thing to confess Christ as a child at school, but another thing to confess Him when manhood and womanhood has awakened and we are launched upon the wider world. How are we to tide young folk over their adolescent years? The Church has been ingenious and prolific in devising new methods of combining the spiritual with the social in earnest and even desperate attempts to lead young men and women into the reality, vitality and felicity of Christian fellowship. To speak the truth, very many of these attempts have failed because they have tactfully postponed the necessity of decision, or have clouded the issue in a fog of friendliness.

There are two methods of seeking to win young folk to Christ. There is the long way round, which proceeds very cannily with much patience and in earnest hope, holding on to young people through some form of human interest. There is the short way in, which puts the issue clearly to young folk, pointing out that if they are going to be Christians, they cannot forever shelve the challenge and responsibility. They are shown that the Christian way of life is not easy, and as Christians they have often to side with a despised minority, and sometimes stand alone for Christ's sake. Experience shows that the result of either method is the same in the end. One gains no more for Christ the long way round than by the short way in. The test of children's work is whether young people who have professed Christ in childhood definitely choose Him and stand by Him in the later days of youth.

A number of folk within the congregation and without may regard us as narrow-minded. This is no doubt due to the fact that we have tried to establish an evangelical Church, and have attracted some folk who were more narrow-minded than Christian. Most of these have gone, since it was made clear that we would not adopt a narrow party or sectarian line. The young people who gather at Gilcomston are surely as healthy, happy and intelligent as one could find. No narrow rules or taboos are laid down either in public or in private. Young people are trained to give their first loyalty to Christ and to His Church, and, with a sound body of Christian teaching, to go out into the world of work and play, and carve out for themselves by the help of the Spirit a Christian life of service. Thus, within the Church, the sole interest is Christ and His Church, in which young folk are offered the privileges of worship on Sunday, of Bible study on Wednesday, and the privilege of prayer for their fellow young folk on Saturday evening. Especially should young folk of 14 years and upwards make the mid-week service a place of meeting during the week. Some do so, and obviously enjoy it in fellowship with their friends.

The question has been sincerely asked by several who are concerned about the young folk in our Church, 'What are you going to provide for young people who do not, or who will not, come to the Sunday services, the mid-week service, and the Prayer meeting?' The answer is, 'Nothing!' If by adolescence young people have not learned to enjoy the services of the Church, then we have failed, or they have failed. To say that we must provide alternatives for those who have no taste or inclination for what Christ and His Church provides, is an impertinence which insults our Lord Jesus Christ.

If the Gospel were preached and Bible instruction inculcated, in a hard, dry, unattractive manner, there would be some cause to demand a lighter alternative, but that is not the case. Then let all who have influence over youth encourage them to attend two at least of the three services on Sunday (why not three?), and the mid-week service on Wednesday. If the ministry fails in this, it fails indeed, and no amount of financial or numerical prosperity can hide the fact.

There have been times when it seemed that parents

actively or passively encouraged their children to put other things before the Church. It would be a terrible thing if some day it could be said that parents had led their children astray. Yet some parents are so anxious that their children should live life to the full, that they tend to encourage or allow too many amusements. I would plead with parents to encourage their young folk to make the Church the heart and centre of their life. Yet it is doubtful whether they can coax them to do what they themselves fail to do. The maxim 'Don't do as I do, do as I say' has never carried weight with the young. If they do not follow their parents, whom are they to follow?

Yours sincerely,
WILLIAM STILL

7/THANKFULNESS

October 1948

My Dear People,

We have had two Sundays of Thanksgiving. One for the temporal blessings of the Harvest, and one for the spiritual blessings of the Communion of the body and blood of our Redeemer. We should be in a very thankful frame of mind. May we all preserve it.

Sometimes it is not easy to see the blessings, and yet when we think more deeply we know that there are so many that it is difficult to single them out. We take them so much for granted, not always because we are ungrateful, but because the blessings we lack fill our thoughts and discomfit our minds, so that we are unable to think of anything else and our whole outlook becomes distempered and discontented.

If you see the grace of God working in your life, and if you recognize material blessings that have come your way as a consequence, *do not forget to thank Him.* It is *sad* when there is nothing for which we feel grateful to God, but it is *serious* when there *is* something and we fail to show gratitude, and it is *tragic* when we are so busy asking for more that we forget to thank Him for what we have received.

Let us consider. The primary reason why God blesses us at all is that He may *enjoy* our thanksgiving and praise. We all like to be thanked and praised, although we do not always deserve it. God likes it more, and He always deserves it. He loves to hear us lisp our praise and gratitude. We do not know why He bothers with us at all, but He does. Surely we are not wrong in saying that, next to the pleasure God has in His dear Son, is the pleasure He has in the sons and daughters who have been begotten through Christ.

How grieved He must be when He hears us praising this one and that one of the frail and fallible sons of men, with never a word for Him for His boundless, matchless grace! Is He not a jealous God? Although He is so generous to us in the friends and loved ones He gives us, yet He jealously seeks the first place in the thoughts of our mind, and in the affections of our heart.

God never tires of giving. Even when we are not grateful, He gives and gives, and gives again. Sometimes when others have grieved Him, as we think, we suppose that God will visit them, punish them or deal hardly with them. Instead He lavishes more tokens of His love upon them, not only that He might *win them*, but also that He might *teach us* to be more forbearing and long-suffering.

Yet God will give nothing in the ultimate sense to the ungrateful heart. The material gifts which He showers upon us may be appreciated for themselves, but it is only when we know and love the Giver that they take on a value beyond their own. What does the hymn say?

Heaven above is softer blue,
Earth around is sweeter green;
Something lives in every hue,
Christless eyes have never seen;

Birds with gladder songs o'erflow,
Flowers with deeper beauties shine,
Since I know, as now I know,
I am His, and He is mine.

Have we missed the love and peace and joy of God because we have failed to give thanks? Is that why our Christian life lacks lustre?

Most of our blessings from God come to us through others. We must thank them too. Not gushingly (they would not like that), but with warm and chaste sincerity. This is an age of gross ingratitude. They say that courtliness, manners and gratitude went out with the Victorians. 'People don't expect that sort of thing today, we are much too matter-of-fact!' Too true, but notice their glad surprise when they meet it. These things may have gone out with the Victorians, but they did not come in with them. They came in with Him who in His Person is 'full of grace and truth' and *He never goes out*. He abides for ever. He is not a fashion. He is eternal. And His manners are not a fashion. They are the expression of the heart and mind of the Eternal.

But let us be very practical. You said grace before that lovely dinner. Have you expressed thanks to the one who planned, provided and cooked it? When you visit your friends, and they have spent time, thought, ingenuity and means to provide a worthy meal, do you walk out and never say 'Thank you?' It was in the little things that men saw the face of God in Jesus. In Him, nothing is little. The cup of cold water is the expression of the Eternal, and the *words of thanks* for the cup of cold water also.

Lest we forget, let us review our day before we sleep each night and see how often we have failed to thank God, and man, for blessings received.

Yours sincerely,
WILLIAM STILL

8/DAYS OF PRAYER

July 1951

My Dear Members and Friends of Gilcomston,

It is increasingly clear, in the forward march of the work of God in our midst, that prayer has become the main spring of the Church. For six years we have sought to put God's Holy Word, the Bible, in its right and proper place, and we have certainly become a Bible-teaching Church. But now, although we have never neglected prayer, nor have we any intention to put aside God's Holy Book, we are beginning to be dominated by the masterful spirit of prayer, and we know that this is the stage penultimate to the sovereign down-coming of God the Holy Ghost in mighty power.[1]

[1] These words were written at a time of unusual spiritual excitement. During this period an opportunity was given, at the close of the evening services, for those who wished to reconsecrate their lives to Christ to stand forward. Each Sunday some did so—on occasions a handful, at other times up to sixty. Later in the year this fruitfulness continued more quietly, and the Church came to believe that 'the revival we sought for was, according to our own prayer, given so quietly that "no man should be in danger of taking the glory"'. The sense of expectation in 1951 was probably heightened by reports in 1950 from the Island of Lewis of spiritual awakening. Two different views of the events in Lewis may be found in *The Diary of Kenneth MacRae,* 1980, pp.443–447. Iain H. Murray (ed.).

In addition to almost three hours of prayer on Saturday evenings and three-quarters of an hour before the evening service on Sundays, we are now opening the Church from 7 a.m. until late evening each day. All Churches should, doubtless, be open all day and every day. Yet it is not primarily to offer any one opportunity to pray that we open our Church (although obviously anyone *is* welcome to worship in God's House), but that those in our congregation and others in sympathy might come to pray for revival in our congregation and city. Intercessors may kneel at the front of the Church (where a Word for each day is indicated in the Bible provided) or may sit in the pews. At 7 p.m., the Church will be closed, and prayer transferred to the Session House where, it is hoped, each evening some will come to pour out their hearts to God. Christians are asked to use these facilities intelligently, seeking God's guidance, and it is particularly hoped that in the evenings free use may be made of the Word of God to confirm faith in the faithfulness of God to His promises.

Not a few earnest Christians have found, during these last two weeks, that the discipline of praying for an hour or two in silence has exposed to them the ineffectualness of their former prayers. Especially in the earlier stages of intensive prayer it may be found that an hour of waiting may elapse before the blessing of God, which makes us loath to depart, comes. This does not mean that we are to allow a procession of irrelevant thoughts to flit through our minds. Use of the Scriptures will keep us to the point. But it *takes time to pray*, and those who are asking for nothing short of full-scale, Holy Ghost revival *must pray much* if they are ever to believe that the blessing will come.

Those who have made use of the House of Prayer will be able to testify, (although it is not a thing to be spoken easily about) that they have found a delight in prayer which has ravished their hearts, and which makes them long and crave, hunger and thirst, for more and more fellowship with the Lord Himself, even if there were no other motive for praying. May we respectfully congratulate those who have found their chiefest joy here in these days.

Beloved Christian friends, keep believing. A tenacious hold of the faithful promises of God will deal with every doubt and fear, and God will give us *increasingly* the spirit of faith and prayer. We shall yet see in Scotland an outpouring of God's Spirit which will make the Revivals of the past seem small in comparison. This statement will be received with derision by worldlings, and alas, by many Christians, but we prefer to seize upon the verse which says:

Faith, mighty faith, the promise sees,
And looks to that alone,
Laughs at impossibilities,
And cries, It shall be done!

Lord, I believe.

Yours sincerely,
WILLIAM STILL

9/GRATITUDE FOR ANOTHER'S MINISTRY

August 1951

My Dear Members and Friends of Gilcomston,

My chief impression on returning home has been of the blessings you have had this past month under the ministry of Professor Finlayson.[1] We are glad that so many have shared this blessing, and not a few have stored, not only in note-books, but in heads and hearts, the rich treasures which he has unearthed from the Divine Word. It has been recognized that a master was in our midst, one who is not only master of several gifts, but is most master in the gracious balance of them all. And yet he has been much more than master minister, he has been such a kind friend. How many of the humblest in our midst have savoured the charm of his personality, for he has given himself without stint to every need, and has left behind him a fragrance of Christ which will have lasting effect upon many, and has earned for him a permanent place in the heart's affections of a multitude who have sumptuously fed upon the finest of the wheat! Words of thanks and expressions of gratitude can be so glib that we hesitate to dismiss one so valued with a pittance of thanks, *but we do wish him to know that we are grateful from our very hearts, for he has done our souls a permanent service. We know that his response will be, 'All glory be to God on high,' and it is because this is the sort of man he is, that we love him so.*

And now, what of the future? For my part I return rested and refreshed, although I must confess that it took me a fair part of the holiday to get rid of the strain enough to relax and enjoy days of leisure. There has been much reflection, and a quite surprising revelation of how much my own spiritual life depended upon the dear praying fellowship at Gilcomston. In one sense I feel quite impoverished and hungry for it again. While reflection revealed many mis-

[1] Gratitude for the ministry of others, and recognition of their gifts, is an essential part of Christian fellowship. This letter marks such appreciation in its comments on the month of the ministry which Professor Roderick A. Finlayson, of the Free Church College, Edinburgh exercised in Gilcomston South in July 1951.

takes, faults and failings in the past year, yet the conviction has grown that we have been on God-given lines, and what we need in the future is just more of what we have been receiving. So far from feeling that the past ministry has been too radical, I genuinely feel that it has not been radical enough. If we are to follow Jesus into all that He has for us, and, please God, for our nation and the world, in these days, we shall have to prepare ourselves for even greater sacrifices of the flesh and of legitimate human pleasures, that God may deeply bless His Church, and break open the hard core of wickedness in this benighted generation.

Many are still to go on holiday, and it will be at least another month before we shall be all together again in the battle, but my thoughts must turn instantly to the winter and its work, and I am glad that I have this month of August to wait upon God and hear what He will say. I shall do so with great expectancy, for I know that He has not taken us thus far for nothing! He that hath ears to hear, let him hear.

Yours in tender love, and in grateful regard for all that you mean to me, and to the Lord's work,

Yours sincerely,
WILLIAM STILL

10/IS OUR ARMY TOO LARGE?

June 1952

Dear Members and Friends of Gilcomston,

By now most holiday plans will be laid and preparations begun! We pray that God will give many bright and sunny days to refresh us after a year of toil and care. At the same time the warmer days and long light mornings and evenings make life easier than in the cold dark night of winter, and no doubt this ease brings its spiritual responsibility with it. If God eases somewhat the strain of life for us He certainly does not intend us to grow slack. Yet this is what summer time does to many Christians. True, we see so little of the sun and have so few really warm days that when the sun shines it is liable to go to our head; but is this not part of the great temptation to draw us away from the Crucified? Will any Christians say that they ever left with a feeling of dispeace and dissatisfaction a real prayer meeting in which their heart was praying to, and praising, the Lord? Yet how often we return from our summer jaunts and holiday excursions (if we would admit it) with a dreadful feeling of flatness, as if to say, 'Well, that's that!' even if our lips say to those who ask us, 'Yes, I enjoyed myself.' It is often a lie, although we see it to be a lie only when we permit ourselves to steal a glance at the Crucified. But that we are too proud to do when we have earnestly planned a 'pleasure' and it has turned out hollow. What is there about a fine day, beautiful scenery, congenial company that can compare with converse with Jesus? Do we despise these gifts of God? No, but neither do we prefer them to Him. The whole point about Jesus is that He is *more than all,* and it is this that should make us dissatisfied with anything other than Him. 'Were the whole realm of nature mine, that were a present far too small.'

The trouble with us in Gilcomston is that we have been fed far too fully on the Word of God by comparison with the slight effect it has had upon us. We suffer so intensely from spiritual indigestion that we have developed some of the nausea that inevitably comes to those who keep sitting at a loaded table long after they have had enough. Not that it is wrong to feed ourselves well, but it is wrong to keep sitting. *God intends food to be strength for work,* and our work is holiness, faithful witness and war for the souls of men. Less theory perhaps and more practice! If the ministry closed down for a time, or we were all scattered from each other and from Christian fellowship, or were thrust into some heathen land where there was no true believer to speak to at all, or if the Russians came and made us slink to a Bible-reading or prayer-meeting in fear of our lives, we might begin to appreciate the privileges God has given us, and begin to enquire *why* He chose to give them to us at all.

God has called us to a special work, that of laying ourselves at His feet to burn out with passion to Him for lost Aberdeen. You may say that is not special to us, it is the work of all Christians. We agree, the call is not special to us. But the response seems to be. At least our response to God's call seems to be unusual enough for even Christians to think us queer. Yet what a tragedy it would be if we heroically stepped forward to obey God's call to 'full-time prayer' without counting the cost of going right on. We are sure to come to the end of human endurance, and it looks as if too many Christians in our midst have come to the place where they have said within their hearts, 'Enough! I can go no further, it is too much to expect!' Yet we have only been going on together for seven short years, whereas many Christians have had to pray from twenty-five to forty years for revival. We hope and believe to see it long before that; but if our call to prayer is part of God's larger strategy for our land, or the world, then it may well take longer, and we *must* persevere. Not only so; but while God sends revival that many may be swept into His kingdom, it is the preparation He seeks for us.

To prepare our hearts for revival is to prepare for heaven, so that in a true sense we can say preparation for revival *is* revival. If the dear people who have committed themselves to God to pray for it do not already feel all this so keenly upon their consciences that it overrides every other consideration and drives them to prayer although there were no Minister at all, then what good will it do his trying to whip them up to it? Can it be that God desires a weeding out even yet? Is our army too large? Read Judges chapter seven if you think this a mad suggestion. If those who are to endure to the end are reduced even to twenty or twelve, then may God bring us together quickly that we may begin to get down to the colossal task. For let us never forget that the world is sitting on a heap of atom bombs ready to go off.

Anyone who gives himself wholly to the Lord for prayer in these times should know that he is linking himself with coming events far beyond the scope of his imagining. Who is sufficient for these things? None of us by ourselves! But we are *not* by ourselves. God has given Himself wholly to us for this purpose and we have Calvary in our hearts. It should be much easier for us to go forward than it was for Jesus; yet He never faltered.

May *we* never falter.

Yours sincerely,
WILLIAM STILL

11/WHAT DO WE 'TELL SCOTLAND?'

April 1954

Dear Members and Friends,

Most of you will have read in the press of Dr Billy Graham's coming to London. Some are not interested in evangelism, and may have dismissed him as an emotional American; but did you know that reputable journals and journalists who had written disparagingly of him before he arrived have, on meeting him and hearing him preach, apologized? This only emphasizes that since Dr Graham began his Crusade practically all Press comment has been favourable. It would therefore appear that evangelism is on the way to becoming respectable, and even popular again, in our day! The time may come when it will be unseemly to make cheap sneers at the Gospel, and we may find our national figures for Church attendance rocketing from the miserable and disgraceful 2 per cent to 10 per cent, to the current American figures of somewhere around 50–60 per cent. Then the Gospel may become front-page news, and reach the headlines.

But evangelism is already creeping into the 'News' in Scotland.

With regard to 'Tell Scotland', we of Gilcomston embrace gladly this opportunity to help quicken our beloved land to the Gospel, and we rejoice that this new movement in evangelism has the official blessing of our Church and General Assembly.[1] At the same time we cannot restrain a wry smile when we hear so many talking about Prayer and Bible Reading and Witnessing now, when we have been trying for years by word and deed to show that this (and not Church hall entertainment) was the Church's real task. Many are now agog with this new idea, its slogans, jargon and techniques, because it has become 'the thing'. Nor are we sorry that this is so, we have been privately for it. But we think it should be recorded that our glad participation in 'Tell Scotland' springs not merely from General Assembly injunctions and recommendations, nor from high-pressure sponsoring by those most intimately concerned for the success of this new project, but because we have been saying, doing and advocating this for years, according to the unchanging command of our Lord in His Word. We believe

[1] 'Tell Scotland' was a movement intended to mobilize the Churches for the evangelizing of the nation.

that this is worth noting. If the Church had always kept close to its Bible, it would never have needed to come back to itself.

For the Church of any day or nation to think that its life and health depend upon stratagems and movements, is to fail to see that all that it needs in any age and place is there, once and for all, in the Bible. All else needed is the Spirit of God blowing through the clean lives of its ministers and taking up the living words of Scripture to send them home to hearts prepared by prayer.

But there are many, and not only in Scotland, who have seen quite plainly that God has prospered us materially and spiritually in Gilcomston because of our return to Scriptural principles, who yet declare and demonstrate that they will have nothing to do with our ways. But they will yet see that if they want their people to open their hearts, not to say their pockets, and become real Christians, some of whom at least may inhabit the manses of Scotland and the mission fields of the world, there is no other way but for the Church to become *itself* again, even though it should lose the support and approval of the vast number of worldly hangers-on who impede its spiritual progress.

Now it is all very well to enthuse about a movement and a slogan, but what are we to *tell* Scotland? As the movement has been conceived it has three stages: to ministers and elders themselves, to the congregation, and to the parish. We are now at the first stage, and it is well that we ask ourselves what we are going to tell the people. We are going to open our Bible with a new incentive, but are we going to open them with unprejudiced eyes? The trouble too often with the Christian Church has been that it has 'interpreted' the Bible, instead of letting it speak for itself. We know that there are wide fields for interpretation, in the Scriptures (prophecy, for instance), but even there, as in all other fundamental matters, the necessary facts stand out clear and plain for all with unjaundiced eyes to see. Do we really believe the Bible sufficiently to let it speak for itself? Is it our intention so to read and expound it that our people may know the whole truth and receive it in true biblical balance?

If the present climate of theological opinion and biblical scholarship is to prevail, we fear that it is going to take many so long to determine what they do believe and what they do not, that this generation may have passed into the Hell about which the modern Church is so uncertain, before they can make up their minds. It is the problem of this, the problem of that—all problems, no solutions; all fog and darkness, no light! And, in any case, where is the apostolic conviction to come from in a Gospel of shreds and patches? It is the surrender of the will to intellectual conviction of the Truth which alone inflames men's hearts and sets them on fire for God. The Gospel will never again run through Scotland and 'set the heather on fire' until the men of the Church of Scotland sacrifice their pride of intellect and fall humbly before Him whose Word is too great for us ever fully to understand, and then rise to proclaim it simply like faithful errand boys. Heralds do not need great intellects (indeed too much may mar their service!). The defence of God's Word is with God. He will look after that! The proclamation of it is with us, and woe betide us if we fail! For if we do, God will find Himself a living Church elsewhere, and by it He will work, and will by-pass us to our everlasting shame. 'All Scripture is God-breathed' says Paul to Timothy, 'and is profitable'. No Christian needs more than this to make him an authoritative herald of God's Word, nor is there any call to jettison his intellect. He will need it, *all* of it, to understand what he has first believed, for 'if any man will *do* his will', says Jesus of His Father, 'he shall *know* the doctrine. . . .' 'The authority of the Holy

Scripture', says our Westminster Confession of Faith, 'for which it ought to be believed and obeyed, dependeth not upon the testimony of any man or church, but wholly upon God (who is Truth itself), the Author thereof; and therefore it is to be received, because it is the Word of God'.

May God grant us all to be so convinced, cleansed and inspired by His Word ourselves, that we proclaim it with convicting and converting power, to His glory, not ours.

Yours earnestly,
WILLIAM STILL

12/QUESTIONS FOR AN ABSENT CONGREGATION

May 1954

Dear Members and Friends,

On Tuesday, 20th April, we gathered to give an official welcome home to Miss Irene Davidson, after five years of missionary teaching and battling against Romanism in Arequipa, inland Peru. I say 'we', for we cannot say 'the congregation': It was conspicuous by its absence. Granted Miss Davidson was a stranger to most of us, but she worked in Church of Scotland circles in Aberdeen until she went abroad, and since we had already welcomed her parents into our fellowship, we thought it not too much to expect a goodly company of our congregation to 'spare' an evening to meet and hear one who with professional qualifications had given up all to follow Christ. But no!

The Minister has often been charged with perpetuating and even widening the gap between old and new Gilcomston. He has not done so, but only exposed it. But it makes him tremble to think that people who have seen what God can do before their very eyes should turn such a deliberately blind eye to God's work, and he can hardly be sorry that they will have to answer for it (if they do not repent) to the God whom they have slighted in His servants.

But the (professedly!) evangelical element was almost as conspicuous by its absence. Where were you, hundreds who profess to be converted and to have the interests of God's kingdom at heart? Many of you had no intention of coming. Why not? There was no tea; there were no jokes; there was no sentimental singing; just an account of the astounding workings of God in South America. It is quite clear that there is a considerable company of so-called evangelicals in our city, as in others, whose interest in Christian work largely depends upon its 'Christian' entertainment value, and who idolize Christian personalities in much the same way as the world does its actors and sportsmen. Even in gatherings for the deepening of spiritual life one can sense and see people hanging on a speaker's words, waiting for his first joke. They wait long sometimes, with sinking hearts, and if eventually they see that like Nehemiah he is too busy to 'come down' (Nehemiah 6:3), they settle themselves to endure it, and hope that the next speaker will be 'better', or they don't go back!

I have often quoted (or paraphrased from memory) the last sentence of Chesterton's book *Orthodoxy*, in which he says there was one element in the character of Jesus which was concealed in the Gospels: 'I have sometimes fancied that it was His mirth'. I feel sure he is right. No one doubts that our Lord was intensely human, and had a glorious sense of humour, but *it is largely concealed* in the Word! And rightly so, for no one who has caught the heart-beat of the eternal God in the agony of Calvary and who is called to communicate the Word will have time or inclination to be any other than intensely serious. Paul and Peter frequently affirm that we must be *sober-minded*! Away then, with all this silly theatrical display of human personality in Christian work, and let us rather wait to weep than laugh. There is need of it today! And yet, the opposite of carnal frivolity is not always tears, but often radiance. Last Sunday morning the text was, 'Let the dead bury their dead: but go thou and preach the kingdom of God', and the preacher was amazed at the number in Church who hung their heads.

Were they ashamed of him, or of Jesus, or of themselves? Even at the last hymn some looked positively miserable, when they should have been singing their hearts out at the sheer thrill of following Christ. Why not?

Yours sincerely,
WILLIAM STILL

13/JOY THROUGH SURRENDER

August 1954

My Dear Friends,

Those who attended the July Sunday evening services noticed that as the unexpected series of early Genesis 'readings' developed, special emphasis was laid upon some words in Genesis 2:9: 'And out of the ground made the Lord God to grow every tree that is pleasant to the sight, and good for food'. We have rejoiced that ours is not a utilitarian God who wants to pare man's life to bare necessities, but one who loves to lavish bounteous gifts.

This is a lesson we find hard who have been taught to mortify the flesh and fleshly things; yet learn it we must, if we would grow in grace. But let us put it in context: we must take up our cross daily and follow, cost what it will. And cost it will, there is no doubt. But when our Lord has bound us fast to His own blessed cross, there is no gift or blessing, lawful and expedient, which He will not bestow upon His willing children to enrich their lives. But let no one think he can *use* consecration to this end. The end is consecration, whether it leads to service or sacrifice; the blessed 'extras' of His love are all of sovereign grace. But when we live the 'cross' life, we see every gift as unmerited bounty, for which we thank Him with spontaneous gratitude. And such a life is ever praising God, for there is no end to the increase of His goodness.

The twofold joy which is ours in seeing fresh young life yielding itself to God in full and glad surrender is too little known. Only when youthful hearts are crucified do we see this and recognize it by the love-light in their eyes and the warmth and reverence in their voices, and in that indefinable 'something' which emanates from youth who have been gloriously captivated by the Saviour's love. It is unmistakable. Happy is he who, having seen its throes and travail, waits to see its birth and growth and glory in the young. But '*twofold* joy' we said: what is the other fold? It is the joy of seeing God's gracious plan unfold for them, opening their way and smoothing difficulties, not least in leading them (not all of them!) to their life's destiny in terms of wedded fellowship. It has been said we would have everyone in splendid isolation because this was God's will for us.[1] This has been, and ever will be, proved untrue. For never more than when two Christian hearts are joined in one by Christ do we enjoy the blessed Spirit's presence.

'All this, and heaven too', may well be said by those who, taking Jesus at His word, have found His cross the place of richest blessing.

[1] The allusion is to his own bachelorhood.

May this continue and increase, and many more be found to prove it true!

Yours ever, to this end,
WILLIAM STILL

P.S. It would be cruel to leave the others out of this. The unrelieved cross you bear may be your preparatory testing time. If not, it will be worth your while in heaven to have borne it to life's end. The gratitude alone of those who will be blessed through you will be sufficient reward.

14/LET PEACE RULE!

March 1956

Dear Christian Friends,

I cannot easily forget how the Spirit of God enlarged my heart on recent Wednesdays as we spoke together on that imperative word in Colossians 3:15, 'Let the peace of Christ rule in your hearts, to which also ye are called in one body; and be ye thankful'. I am assured that it was a spiritual landmark to several. It was the emphasis the Spirit enabled us to put upon the word 'rule' that was remarkable, and also the stress that was laid upon the necessity of peace as the foundation of the Christian life. But, somehow or the other, it seems too big a thing to be able to say so simply, namely, that *the supreme test of the Christian life is peace*. Yet, there it is, for those who can receive it.

Many Christians seem to think that the concept of peace is too passive and negative to bear such weight of Christian importance. But is it? It certainly does not suggest action to busy spirits who like to be in the thick of getting things done. But it depends on what we mean by getting things done. Busy people get outward things done, but are these the things that most need to be done?

It cannot be too often repeated that the Holy Spirit is God's *only Worker*. It is true that He chooses to work through His children, but our part is not the co-operation of *help* so much as that of *willing consent*. And even if we rate it higher, it is always *His* will that is done, and *His* power that it is done by, however active we seem to be. Otherwise it is not done at all. God's blessings flow down to us through pipes empty and clean. Now a pipe, to form a channel, must not elect to stand upon its end to see and be seen, but lie down in the muck and be covered over and forgotten. And every time we turn on a water tap, we should be grateful for the pipes that lie buried in the ground. Similarly our active part is to lie low, and *let* God work through us.

This being so, how deep is the lesson of peace we have to learn! Since God is willing and eager to be at peace with us (on His terms, of course!) about anything in heaven and earth or hell, there is therefore nothing in the whole wide world that should disturb us. When we are there, we are founded on rock, for our peace is built upon *His sure Word*. Let us ask ourselves the question, Can we do *more* than He wills? We only need to ponder His astonishing ingenuity in queering our pitch and foiling our crafty purposes to know that man can never hope to do what God forbids. Let us also ask, Can man or demon harm the child of God whom He promises to protect? We only need to review how often in our lives all seemed lost, and God stepped in, and quietly reversed the calamity that threatened, to be assured that there is *nothing* to fear.

Not much wonder, then, that our smiling Father God puts on a grim face here and sternly commands in the imperative mood, 'Let the peace of Christ *rule* in your hearts'! for this is the beginning and ending of everything, in Christian life and service.

Let . . . peace . . . rule!
Yours, to this end,
WILLIAM STILL

15/SALVATION'S THIRD DIMENSION

September 1956

Dear Christians,

It is sometimes said that salvation has three tenses—past, present, and future. Not so often do we hear that salvation has three dimensions, but this is also true, and of vast practical importance. Toplady in his hymn, *Rock of Ages,* indicates the first two dimensions in his comprehensive line about sin, 'Cleanse me from its *guilt* and *power*'. But the third dimension is demonic or Satanic, and we hear very little about that. Yet we must be saved not only from sin's guilt and sin's power, but from Satan also. Why do we hear so little about this? Because it is the devil's concern to keep his existence, presence, and working, secret. He chooses to work in the dark.

God has given us this message, towards his unmasking, and we wish Christians would see that there is no hope of 'peace which passes all understanding' until they have reached the third dimension. But there is prejudice against this teaching, and we can understand why: the subjects of 'sins' and 'sin' are unpleasant, but not uncanny, as is that of Satan. So men remain ignorant of his devices, and give him the licence he wants, which is half his crafty battle.

We believe consecrated Christians are assailed by Satan and his demons. The reason is not far to seek: such Christians have learned to deal with inbred sin, and the enemy has lost his hold upon them, and must needs regain it in some other way. And he is not without stratagem. He invades the life (in the person of a demon or demons) disguised as a revival of inbred sin, and works undetected, with the result that the believer loses faith in the Gospel. Harassed, perplexed and ignominiously defeated, the believer struggles blindly on, cursing his sin, yet unable to break its power in his life, not knowing that it is persons he must deal with, not powers or passions. He needs to know that he is not fighting *sin*, although sin is the battleground, but *Satan* and his demon host. Therefore he must be taught to lay hold upon a greater measure of the power of the death of Christ—its third dimension—to deal with his foe.

This is clear enough, when we see it. But *will* people see it? The purpose of these lines is to help to open our minds to this teaching. But it is just here that the devil is so clever. He is by nature a deceiver, and what better occupation than deceiving men about himself! Men will rather blame themselves for their sin than blame the devil. This they think pious, but who is so 'pious' as the devil himself! And many defeated Christians castigate themselves almost to death, not knowing that Satan lurks securely and undetected, laughing his head off at their self-inflicted punishment. Yet they will not believe. As soon believe that they have cancer or tuberculosis as that they have a demon 'bug'. But in the end it must be faced, for the alternative is destruction, and mental homes are full of people whose lives have thus been virtually destroyed. If we would believe that every example of entrenched evil, where sin is truly hated and yet helplessly succumbed to, is an area of demonic working, there would be some hope of cure. But there can be no cure without a discovery of the cause.

We believe that this mesage should have been delivered years ago, but Satan hindered. But he hinders no longer, although few may understand how bitterly contested these words have been. It may be supposed that our pastoral work has become of a psychological, or rather psychiatric nature; but this is not strictly true. It is spiritual work, although it involves the healing of minds and bodies as well as souls. But its point should not be missed, for health is not the *end*, but the *means* of training in *character* for service.

God purposes a crop of labourers in our midst. That is why our work has been subject to such bitter opposition through the years. Of course we have not been guiltless in the past—Satan has seen to that—but many good people who have been puzzled at the trends and their drastic pruning have not seen, or have not wanted to see, that the ground was being cleared for a major purpose. Some who were formerly opposers have wondered why they felt so incensed against us, and have subsequently admitted that the fury of their anger frightened them. This is the reason: they were the unconscious, although not innocent, dupes of a frantic devil fighting a rearguard action. Now they know.

But the devil is retreating, and will retreat, for God purposes a crop. It remains simply to ask your prayers for the one who is called to lead this enterprise.

Yours sincerely,

WILLIAM STILL

16/THE BLESSINGS OF NATURE

July 1958

My Dear Friends,

I love Psalm 19. Do you know it well? It is the one which begins, 'The heavens are telling the glory of God, and the firmament proclaims his handiwork. Day pours forth speech to day, and night declares knowledge to night. There is no speech, nor are there words; their voice is not heard. Their [sign] language goes out through all the earth, and their [wordless] words to the end of the world'.

Then the sunrise is described thus: 'In them he has set a tent for the sun, which comes forth like a bridegroom leaving his chamber, and like a strong man runs its course with joy. Its rising is from the end of the heavens, and its circuit to the end of them, and there is nothing hid from its heat.'

We have every encouragement, then, from the Word of God to see the glory of God in the wonders of nature. Do you know John Keble's hymn of creation?

There is a book, who runs may read,
Which heavenly truth imparts,
And all the lore its scholars need,
Pure eyes and Christian hearts.

The works of God, above, below,
Within us and around,

Are pages in that book, to show
How God Himself is found.

The glorious sky, embracing all,
Is like the Maker's love,
Wherewith encompassed, great and small
In peace and order move.

The dew of heaven is like Thy grace:
It steals in silence down:
But, where it lights, the favoured place
By richest fruits is known.

One name, above all glorious names,
With its ten thousand tongues
The everlasting sea proclaims,
Echoing angelic songs.

Two worlds are ours; 'tis only sin
Forbids us to descry
The mystic heaven and earth within,
Plain as the sea and sky.

Thou who hast given me eyes to see
And love this sight so fair,
Give me a heart to find out Thee,
And read Thee everywhere.

It is a growing conviction with us that holiday time, which is a necessity to those who would maintain a busy life efficiently, needs to be a time of rest, and re-creation. No environment offers more hope of this than that which gets back as nearly as may be to nature. By that we mean that those who spend their lives in the confined and artificial environment of man-made city life should choose a holiday which offers the greatest possible scope for getting away from man and his inventions, to let God speak afresh through nature.

Think for a moment of the atmosphere of the open spaces, the various music of the winds and waves, the mightier hush of the mystic silence, not to speak of the effect of hill and dale, sea and sky, of sun and moon, of clouds and even haze. Then there is the glorious world of living things, the birds, and beasts and insects, the trees and flowers and grasses, the rocks and contours and rolling farm lands. Although every one does not find pleasure in solitude on holiday, it is alone or with at most a sympathetic and often silent companion that these wonders are best enjoyed.

Some may say these are for imaginative natures only, and staid, prosaic, practical people do not find absorbing and enchanting interest in them. That may be, and more's the pity—all the more reason they should try to cultivate the delicate art of appreciating the free and simple and grand things of life. For some this would require discipline, and unfortunately it is when we are least inclined to yield ourselves leisurely to these delights that our jaded lives are most in need of them. Let us try to wage war against the mechanical superficiality of our urban life, and keep periodical tryst with the life that helped to make our fathers great. For there is no doubt about this, to those who have the Word of God and store it in their minds and hearts, there is no place where it does its deepest work so well as in close contact with nature. On the lonely hillside, or by the babbling brook or seashore, the treasures of God's holy Word will come alive to you again and again, and values, proportions and perspectives will be restored, with a healing and invigorating power that will make you marvel.

Some cannot get away and thereby feel themselves deeply

deprived of life's normal blessings. What can I say to them? Well, if you are laid aside by inability you will not be in such need of restoring rest. It is the change you long for, perhaps the very thing from which the others are running away. Perhaps a trip or two to pastures new, an outing with a change of scene, anything to vary the sight of sticks and stones we gaze upon so much.

The longest holidays are not necessarily the best. If they are too long and the days sprawl on in changeless monotony they will not help, but make us long for the ordered purposefulness of daily life and a job well done again. Even an afternoon, an hour, can contain such intensity of pleasure as far exceeds many days of duller ease. And let us not forget, if we have need of such a lesson, that the sweetest songs that godly poets have sung have been composed on beds in cells and dungeons of the strictest confinement.

The great thing is to be in God's will, so we know we are in the line of His blessing. We shall find this contains more pleasure, whatever it be, than we have ever believed.

Yours sincerely,
WILLIAM STILL

17/THE SABBATH DAY

March 1959

My Dear Friends,

The General Assembly is to be overtured concerning the Christian use of Sunday. In this connection some historical notes and comments have been circulated, upon which we wish to make observations.

The intention of the present action, as far as we can

understand it, is to prevent the alienation from the Church of those who want to use Sunday for both worship and recreation. It is intended to encourage a more positive attitude to the Christian Sunday, whose use, it is said, is threefold: for worship, rest and recreation—recreation being 'harmless pastimes' and 'legitimate enjoyments.'

Does this movement, which is inviting the Church to reformulate her teaching concerning Sunday, arise from popular pressure? We cannot say. It is plain that an attempt has been made to modify the Church's attitude to the Christian Sunday by an appeal to the Bible and Church history, but the impression is also gained that only a popular interpretation will be acceptable!

It has been found, the notes affirm, that in a biblical and historical survey 'Sabbath observance and Lord's Day worship were never thought of as integrally related to each other, even in the period when they were both practised by Christians.' 'The Lord's Day and Sabbath were consistently opposed to each other by Church leaders for four centuries.' The Reformers are also appealed to for similar conclusions, and their teaching summed up thus: 'The fourth Commandment (part of the Old Covenant) was abrogated by the New Testament Scriptures (and the New Covenant).'

These statements have to be challenged. As far as the Bible is concerned there is no shadow of doubt that the Sabbath (first Jewish, then Christian) is of abiding sanction. It is of 'divine origin' and a 'necessity of human nature', and goes back not only to Moses and Sinai, but to Creation. Jesus said, 'the Sabbath was made for man' by which He implied that man has need of a day of rest, one in seven. Nor can there be any doubt that the Christian Sabbath was instituted by God to commemorate the Resurrection, the disciples being led by the Holy Spirit to establish the Lord's Day.

This is not what the writers of these notes believe. 'Unlike the Sabbath, it was not instituted: it just happened'. 'The Resurrection . . . fell on the first day of the week.' It 'happened' and 'fell'. We would hardly like to put it like that! The intention appears to be to separate the Sabbath from the Lord's Day so as to remove the conception of rest from the modern Sunday.

Concerning early Church history, we can understand the tension created between the Jewish Sabbath and the Lord's Day both as to the number of the day and as to the Old and New Covenants. But we have no doubt that the Lord was leading the Church to make the change, with a new orientation, to grace instead of law, and privilege instead of commandment.

Concerning the Reformers it is obvious that a one-sided case has been made out for their attitude to the Christian Sabbath, as is plain from the following quotations from Calvin's *Institutes*. Of the fourth Commandment he says, 'Indeed, there is no commandment the observance of which the Almighty more strictly enforces. . . . The observance of it He eulogises in the highest terms, and hence, among other divine privileges the faithful set an extraordinary value on the revelation of the Sabbath' (*Inst.* II, viii, 29). 'Why should we not adopt the rule which the will of God has obviously imposed upon us? I am obliged to dwell a little longer on this, because some restless spirits are now making an outcry about the observance of the Lord's Day. They complain that Christian people are trained in Judaism, because some observance of days is retained. My reply is, that those days are observed by us without Judaism, because in this matter we differ widely from the Jews. . . . [Paul] tells the Romans that it is superstitious to make one day differ from another (Romans 14:5). But who, except these restless men, does not see what the observance is to which the Apostle refers? Those persons had no regard to that political and ecclesiastical arrangement, but by retaining the days as types of spiritual things, they in so far obscured the glory of Christ, and the light of the Gospel. They did not desist from manual labour on the ground of its interfering with sacred duty and meditation, but as a kind of religious observance; because they dreamed that by their cessation from labour, they were cultivating the mysteries which had of old been committed to them' (*Inst.* II, viii, 32, 33). 'It was not without a reason that the early Christians substituted what we call the Lord's Day for the Sabbath' (*Inst.* II, viii, 34).

Strangely enough the notes quote Chrysostom declaring that 'God from the first teaches us symbolically to set apart one whole day in the week and devote it to spiritual activities'; but this is at once set at naught. Yet the Westminster Confession of Faith after many centuries amplifies and substantiates Chrysostom: 'As it is of the law of nature, that, in general, a due proportion of time has been set apart for the worship of God; so, in His Word, by a positive, moral, and perpetual commandment, binding all men in all ages, He hath particularly appointed one day in seven for a sabbath, to be kept holy unto Him: which, from the beginning of the world to the resurrection of Christ, was the last day of the week; and, from the resurrection of Christ was changed into the first day of the week, which in Scripture is called the Lord's Day, and is to be continued to the end of the world, as the Christian Sabbath' (21:7).

It seems to us that the basic doctrinal error in the new approach is the false distinction between the two Covenants. Nor can we avoid the conclusion that the Reformers' teaching is wrested to set the Covenants at variance. Certainly the Old Covenant is abrogated concerning its commandment and ritual condemnation, but not concerning the provision and privileges which underlie it. Paul, writing to the Romans, provides the bridge between his revolutionary teaching to the Galatians and the Old Testament law, in a working synthesis, when he declares that God sent His Son in the likeness of the flesh of sin to do what the holy, but helpless, law could not do; 'that the *righteousness of the law* might be *fulfilled in us,* who walk not after the flesh, but after the Spirit' (Rom. 8:3–4). And later, 'For Christ is the end of the law for righteousness. . . .' (Rom. 10:4). Not the end of the law, for He came to fulfil every jot and tittle of it, but 'the end of the law *for righteousness*', that is to say, as a means of attaining righteousness. But the righteousness otherwise attained by the Spirit is still the righteousness of the law, not now prescribed, but described. Thus a false antithesis of the Old and New Covenants has been set up.

We know, of course, that ours is a National Church which has a responsibility to the whole community. But it has no duty to un-Church itself at popular request. The Christian Sabbath has become irksome to nominal members of the Kirk who like to pay their morning respects to the Almighty, as the Romans do, and spend the rest of the day as they like. But the Christian Sabbath is not irksome duty. To those who love the Lord (the only category who have a right to sit at the Lord's Table) it arises not primarily from the demand of the ten commandments, holy as they are (Romans 7:12); but from the gracious provision of Genesis 2:3: 'And God blessed the seventh day, and sanctified it.' The privileges of the Christian Sabbath, therefore, are not to be laid alongside the legal demands of the Mosaic law, 'added because of transgressions' (Gal. 3:19); but with the enjoyment of the Gospel as linked by Paul with the promises to Abraham.

Grace before Law provides blessings before commands, as in the Sabbath and Marriage (compare Gen. 2:23, 24 with

Exod. 20:14); and it will never do to filch away our Christian heritage by laying its inconvenient parts under the injunctions of legalism and then throwing them out.

Hear the Westminster Confession again: 'This sabbath is then kept holy unto the Lord, when men, after a due preparing of their hearts, and ordering of their common affairs beforehand, do not only observe an holy rest all the day from their own works, words, and thoughts about their worldly employments and recreations; but also are taken up the whole time in the public and private exercise of his worship, and in the duties of necessity and mercy.'

There are many tensions with which a National Church must grapple, but the solution is never to capitulate to popular and worldly pressure. That way we may remain National, but National what? Not the Church of the Bible and of Christ!

Yours sincerely,
WILLIAM STILL

18/JOSEPH

June 1959

My Dear Friends,

On the conclusion of the Wednesday Bible Studies in Genesis, with the magnificent story of Joseph, it was suggested we had in him a perfect example of the political good a God-fearing man can do for his country. I am impressed with this, and want to say a word about it now.

Joseph became Prime Minister of Egypt, and affected that nation's life (so say the historians) with signs of political sagacity writ plain on history's page for a dynasty at least.

Egypt was a great power when the stripling came to its land, advanced in art and science beyond any nation of the day (see the British Museum). But since civilization depends in the long run on the moral tone of the people, there was much in Egypt that sorely needed a Joseph; and God matched the hour with the man. Yet it is not Joseph's moral integrity which we note first, but the sovereign calling of God, revealed in dreams of his future supremacy. This is the first thing in a life that honours God, that it is called to destiny. We can do nothing about this, but watch and wait, and yet, if we believe in the reality of God's election, we know that He has a place for us, and we shall refuse to be moved by other incentives until His will is made known. When it is, it provides an incentive that heightens the importance of life, and makes quality of thought and character supreme and directive in all matters, great and small.

This is the next thing about Joseph: he was not only called, he was faithful. Even in Potiphar's house, where the standards of conduct were flexible, and where a little passionate licence might be indulged in 'safe' privacy, he was imprisoned for his pains in refusing the advances of a lordly but adulterous wife. And in prison, as at home and in Potiphar's house, he was a man with a mission in life and a spirit of service towards his fellows. There was nothing of corrupting ambition about Joseph. It was his to do right and to do good, wherever he was. He was under authority and obedient to the heavenly vision of his dreams, and as one called to rule was as one called to serve. Only those under divine authority can truly serve.

Yet the plan was long delayed. The forgetfulness of a butler for two long years was surely something the Almighty could have over-ruled. But it is not His will to over-ride the unwieldy material of nature. Though the vision tarry, wait for it; and the butler at last remembered, at the psychological moment of men's need and of Pharaoh's. The prophecy of famine was plain to the man who was in God's will, and with his calling, integrity, and insight came a master plan to avert its worst calamities in a nation soon to shelter the most precious family on earth. There was none in Egypt to put this bold strategy into effect but the man who had seen and declared it. Thus Joseph began to build and buy with a view to a prodigious food bank to save a nation from starvation. Surely Joseph was come to the kingdom, like Esther, 'for such a time as this', and surely God has His men who will rise and devise creative plans for the preservation of a people through whom divine life is to be transmitted!

So Joseph, the called and faithful one, the good and true and discerning, the wise-hearted and clear-headed, became lord of all Egypt. But that is not all. He dealt faithfully with his heartless brothers, and gave them a taste of their own medicine, but in compassion and brotherly kindness. When his father was come to the land of his son's adoption and glory, he made sure his family was given a part of the land where the race could multiply freely and in comparative purity of blood. And when the nobles and wealthy of Egypt were bartering their jewels and cattle and selling their persons for food to keep body and soul together, the favoured children of Jehovah had plenty and were preserved in prosperity and peace. Not that Joseph is heartless with the Egyptians, but he drives a hard bargain to put the nation under the power and possession of Pharaoh. And when Joseph's father is dead, and the brothers fear reprisals for the ill they did in the far-off days of his youth, his grace and forgiveness shine forth in luminous glory as the kindness of Jehovah to him is passed on to his own and his fellows.

We do not know all the sweeping significance of these masterly strokes of Joseph the Statesman. But they minister to the fulness of Jehovah's plan to bring a nation from

Egypt, and in Solomon's days make them the glory of the earth, and in later captivity and shame preserve them a remnant in servitude until He come whose right it is to reign, even the One for whom for generations the holy family was maintained in precarious but invincible life.

Here is a lesson in political responsibility which evangelicals do well to learn. May it be learned by those for whom it is intended, speedily and thoroughly, lest in the end the ministers of God's holy word be distracted from the ministry and prayer, to the serving of tables. The tables must be served, if life is to go on. But the line is not by Joseph, but by Judah, the royal tribe.

Yours sincerely,
WILLIAM STILL

19/TIME

January 1960

My Dear Friends,

It is my pleasure again to wish you all a Happy New Year. May 1960 bring us all nearer to the divine pattern, which is surely our wish for ourselves.

May I also, without obtruding the man, thank all who have taken the opportunity the Christmas season affords to give thanks for another year's ministry. This is pleasing to God and encouraging to me, and is good for those who do it. What if God blesses us in proportion as we thank Him for past blessings! Every smallest deed of kindness this Christmas has brought joy to my heart, and I want to give thanks to God and to you for it all.

Our wish, for us all, this year, is that we may be pleasing to God. This covers everything. There is nothing sanctimonious, and certainly nothing quietist or lugubrious about it: it sets human life at its highest level. Nor is it so high that it is no earthly use; for it is active, positive, constructive, realistic, optimistic, adventurous, heroic, and challenging!

The 90th Psalm which we were reading at the Watch-Night Service, and the paraphrase of it ('O God, our help in ages past') which we sang, may seem to be a little on the pessimistic side. God is set over against man. The Psalmist has no doubt that God will endure: 'Before the mountains were brought forth, or ever Thou hadst formed the earth and the world, even from everlasting to everlasting, Thou art God.' But he is not so sure about man. 'Time, like an ever-rolling stream, bears all its sons away; they fly forgotten as a dream dies at the opening day.' 'As for man his days are as grass. In the morning it flourisheth and groweth up; in the evening it is cut down and withereth. For all our days are passed away in Thy wrath: we spend our years as a tale that is told. For a thousand years in Thy sight are but as yesterday when it is past, and as a watch in the night. Thou carriest them away as with a flood; they are as a sleep. . . . The days of our years are threescore years and ten, and if by reason of strength they be fourscore years, yet is their strength labour and sorrow, for it is soon cut off and we fly away. . . So teach us to number our days that we may apply our hearts unto wisdom.'

But we are not to think of time as an all-prevailing assembly line which masterfully carries us away into meaningless oblivion. Time is not God's master, but His servant. It must be the Christian's servant, too. For it is a creation of God. And the Father has put 'times and seasons' under His own power, for His purposes. If time is an ever-rolling stream, it is not meant to bear us helplessly away as if we were so much useless driftwood; far less are we to try to swim against its tide and defy the forces of nature; but we are to use it as a stream to 'bear us far', 'from out the bourne of time and place'. And, yet, it is the stream on which we are to navigate skilfully and purposefully. We are to use everything that could be against us, as well as all things neutral, to make capital out of them, that all might serve the over-ruling and underlying purposes of God.

God has given us a supply of time, which we are to redeem because the days are evil. John tells us that Satan is ever raging more madly as he sees his time shortening, and many lazy and scatter-brained Christians begin to panic when they see their time is short. We ourselves must find out what God made us for, and then, under His control and not under our own ambition, go ahead and do it with all our might, pressing on, forging ahead, climbing steadily, nothing daunted . . . forgetting those things which are behind, and reaching forward to those things which are before, and pressing towards the goal for the prize of the high calling of God in Christ Jesus. Point, direction, purpose, clear motive, definite aim, and a personality geared to God's will are what we need.

Look at Jesus' thirty-three years of life. Look at His three years of ministry. No life could have been so full of interesting things. But even the healing of the sick had to be set aside for more important things, and the teaching of the twelve had to come to an end, and then, before Him, in the prime of life, was this cruel life-destroying cross. But He faltered not. For the joy that was set before Him He endured the cross, despising the shame, and is seated at the right hand of the throne of God. Consider Him who endured such contradiction of sinners against Himself, lest you be wearied and faint in your minds!

The cross was not something which bore Christ away: it was not a bier, a catafalque, a coffin; but a throne, a chariot, a doorway through which He made His exodus from mortal into immortal life, and passed into glory. And this He did, not only for Himself. 'Thanks be unto God who gives *us* the victory through our Lord Jesus Christ. . . . Therefore my beloved brethren, be steadfast, unmoveable, always abounding in the work of the Lord. For you know that your labour is not in vain in the Lord.'

Time, then, is not something which bears us away, but something upon which we may ride to victory. It is not something which takes us away at all, but something which has to be taken by the forelock and used to God's glory for the present doing of His will.

God uses the evil for His good purposes. We must use time, tide, place, things, and beings, good and bad—even the devil himself—to further the beneficent purposes of God.

Are you riding high on the wings of God's holy purposes? or are you drifting? You must first find your link with God's will. What did He make you for? Then, in His control, go ahead and do it or bear it, with all your might, and you will triumph, even if you come to a martyr's end. For a martyr's end is not a stake, or a cross, or a sword, or a brain-washed nonentity, and then merciful death; but, beyond all these horrors—a crown of glory, 'which fadeth not away, reserved in heaven for you, who are kept by the power of God through faith unto salvation ready to be revealed in the last time. Wherein ye greatly rejoice, though now for a season, if need be, ye are in heaviness through manifold temptations: that the trial of your faith, being much more precious than of gold, which, though it be tried with fire, yet perisheth, might be found unto praise and honour and glory at the appearing of Jesus Christ: whom having not seen, ye love; in whom, though now ye see Him not, yet believing, ye rejoice with joy unspeakable and full of glory: receiving the end of your faith, even the salvation of your souls.'

Yours affectionately,

WILLIAM STILL

20/TRUE REFORMATION COMMEMORATIONS

November 1960

My Dear Friends,

We reach the climax of the Reformation celebrations this month. I do not know if it is my dislike of special events which tend to depreciate the normal and the ordinary, or whether I am faintly cynical about the auspices of the celebrations, but my inclinations are to pay my sincere respects as quickly as possible, and get on with the work.

If we owe anything to the Reformation, let us speedily and permanently incorporate it into the life and work of the Church. That will be a better memorial than tablets or meetings or ceremonial occasions. We are not saying the occasion should not be marked, but wonder if it is those who are most inspired by Reformation principles who are keenest on its commemoration. We wonder if important public figures are not secretly embarrassed sometimes by the tensions presumably created in their minds by the contradictory causes they sponsor. Do stout Reformation principles and shallow Ecumenicity (a World Church under one Organization) go together? Or is it that we stretch a point here and there to suit the times and occasion, until we are so much of everything that we are not much of anything at all? Are we so chameleon-like that we turn up in any company and in any 'garb' to give unctuous support to almost any cause—even an atheist's memorial service in Westminster Abbey? Perhaps Princess Margaret's long journey from Scotland to attend an ordination service is not so encouraging after all when it is so closely associated with the man who gave that disgraceful eulogy of an unbeliever from the Abbey pulpit. Surely if a man is honest enough to forbid Christian prayers at his funeral, it ill-becomes his Christian friends sentimentally to foist a faith upon him at his demise! But that was in England! Yet in Scotland also there are influences that are just as alarming.

And we can pay too much heed to a point of time, and, possibly, also to great figures of the past, and be so dwarfed by them that we fail to rise to our own Reformation. For Reformation is a constant process in a living Church. Do we ever meet in worship without seeking renewal by the Holy Ghost, with all that that involves? Even a sincere desire to return to the Reformation principles of the past could be inadequate and frustrating, for the process of renewal has gone many cycles in four hundred years, and the emphasis today may need to be different from the emphasis then. The Church is growing, not only in numbers in heaven, but, we trust, in insight on earth (not beyond the Scriptures, but into them); and we should return to our foundations neither with hypocritical adulation nor fixated veneration, but with a view to running our eye up the house we are building to see if it is plumb on the line our fathers left. It is therefore not only back to the Scottish Reformation, but to the Continental Reformation, too, and to every true Reformation that stemmed from the Word of God. Indeed, only a return to the Word of God will give the impulse towards further Reformation, and, with the wisdom of the Christian centuries behind us, drive us on towards the heavenly kingdom God is secretly building by His Church.

If this celebration does any lasting good, it will be in the ordinary life of the Church. If that does not become more Christian, and increase our godly impact upon the Church and the world, it is no more than a ceremonial diversion graced with royal recognition and punctuated by fine speeches. We are not against either, but if the Church is to be no better for it in every city and town and hamlet of our land, it is not of much importance.

Servants of God who revere the Word of God and His living Spirit in the Church need no commemorations to encourage them. They are living in the atmosphere of renewal and reform and should be ever attuning their minds and hearts to what the Lord is saying in their age and day. Those Romanists who worship a dead Christ, cart their images round in procession occasionally, lest religion die and the priesthood become redundant. We need no such 'aids', only a baptism of reality to recapture the glory of the ordinary in the service of God. We need nothing new, but that which is 'new every morning'.

Yours sincerely,
WILLIAM STILL

21/REBUILD THE CHURCH!

November 1960

My Dear Friends,

The following are the Notes of an address given by me at a meeting of the Baptist Ministers' Fellowship, held during the Scottish Baptist Assembly in Aberdeen, 24th–27th October.

My Brothers, I would like to speak to you about the ageless things of our Christian faith, which evangelical fashions, just as much as any other fashions in Christendom, are likely to cloud over and conceal, to the detriment of the Church of our day, to the decline of its true nature and growth, and to the failure of its impact upon the nation and nations, and the loss of its preservative and cleansing power in the societies of men.

We often hear the Church's dual tasks—of teaching its own and preaching to others—pitted against each other, or set in priority over one another. Of the different arguments which rage over this question of evangelism versus edification, the one I consider most serious and hazardous to the Christian cause is that which says that the Christian Church's chief task, or even sole task, is evangelism, the great commission in the Gospel by Matthew being quoted in support.

I think we have to be careful here. Those who have been most involved in evangelism know best that it is exhausting work, and many of God's servants have exhausted themselves in it. Like youth work, it is a most exacting and arduous form of service, which takes all the greater toll of our total powers because it is constantly making appeal to the generally indifferent mass of humanity. But, you may say, that is no reason for dispensing with it because it is costly. But the reason why it is so costly is that, divorced from the total life of the Church, it tends to go out on a limb of the Christian tree and wave itself almost off the trunk, until it loses all relation to God's overall purpose. But what are we seeking to do? Save or win the world, or prepare for Christ's Kingdom by calling out and building up His Church? The answer we give to that question matters a great deal. We are perhaps far too eager, optimistic, and active. Now, this may seem to be the veriest heresy to some of you men, but it could hardly be said that I am inactive, or that I am not concerned for fruitfulness.

The Church's first task, it seems to me, is to *keep being herself* in a changing world, and thus to build herself up and fortify herself against the growing onslaughts of evil, as prophesied in history and in each successive generation.

This she can only do by being, not evangelically minded, devotionally or convention minded, socially minded, ecumenically minded, or politically minded; but by taking the whole Word of God as her diet, and feeding and building herself up on that. Thus she preserves her strength for every heroic task, including all these, and makes impact, often painful impact, upon all the life of her day. To this end I think we all, without respect of denomination, need to dismantle our Churches, congregation by congregation, right down to the stocks. Then we must build them up again upon a more severe pattern, and strictly on the one unchangeable foundation of Jesus Christ, in order to meet the challenge of our day.

Now, I do not believe that this will carry everyone's judgment, but for the sake of argument (just to hear what this babbler will say!) let us in imagination take our own congregation down, stop all meetings, activities, organizations, clubs, socials, until there is nothing left but an empty building, and an undifferentiated group of people—all segregation of age groups, Sunday School apart, being abolished—who owe some kind of allegiance to Jesus Christ in that particular place. What are you going to do? What are to be your foundations? What are to be your bare priorities? What is the life of the Christian congregation? It is the indwelling, unifying and incorporating Spirit of Christ. What is its sustenance? It is the Word of God. How is the Word of God to be ministered so that it becomes the spiritual bone, flesh, and life-blood of God's people? The Word must become flesh again, as it did in Christ, and that flesh must die the death to self, which is so costly, for 'except a corn of wheat fall into the ground and die, it abideth alone; but if it die, it bringeth forth much fruit.' We must digest our Lord's stark words: 'If any man hate not . . . he cannot be my disciple.' And that Word of God, broken down by the Spirit, and made spiritually edible and assimilable by the devoted labours of God's called and consecrated servant, and by the prayers of His expectant and believing people, will find lodgment, any kind of lodgment —from a barb to a caress—in the hearts of the saints. In this way the Church of Jesus will become a living thing, all untrammelled by time-consuming and dreary organization, from which all sorts of potentialities, both gracious and explosive, will emerge. A hungry people, an anointed man, the Word of God, the Spirit's breath in prayer and worship and spiritual fellowship, the water, bread and wine—you need nothing else to form a Church that will come alive and alight, and glow and burn and flame its way through a community and people and nation, until by spontaneously improvised strategies it makes its way to the uttermost parts of the earth.

Is this our Church? If not, what use are all our activities? Shall I tell you what will be the fruits of such rigorous concentration and simplification as I suggest? People will be converted, and people will become mad. Some that are converted and many that are not will alike become mad; but at least a tiny nucleus will be built up in the faith and find their own spontaneous expressions of service. You will not have to organize them; and if some depart, others will take their place, to whom the freshness of the Word of God winged by the prayers of the saints and by the Spirit of God will become the most sensational and heart-warming news to thrill their new-born souls. They will delve deeper into their pockets without any one telling them, and the offerings will swell, and the question on everyone's heart and mind will be: Lord, what wilt thou have me to do? Social pastoral work, mere polite visitation, will be largely submerged by vital dealing with souls. The fascination of the power of the Word of God preached simply in the Spirit will altogether preoccupy God's servant: his priorities will radically change, and he will be sought out by those who would discuss with him the practical (sometimes painfully practical) implications of the preaching and teaching of the Word of God. He will soon be obliged to take an interest in Christian work in lands and places and stations other than his denomination may be working in, as the Spirit thrusts out his young people into the four corners of the earth, and he finds like John Wesley that almost overnight the world has become his parish.

Is this a dream and an exaggeration? I do not believe it is for me to be more specific, lest I in anywise abuse or take advantage of your brotherly hospitality, but I can tell you that the beginnings of such a work are taking place today, in your denomination and in mine. But some may say, What of the rest of the Church? All our multifarious activities and agencies? Well, what about them? What more is there, and what need of more, when such bare priorities have so potent an effect? A bare foundation? There is nothing bare about the Word of God when the Spirit brings it home in its fulness, sweetness, power and effect. This is the Church: worshipping, praying, receiving the living Word. The rest is frills and largely fruitless dissipation of effort, body and soul, a weary and wearying round that wears us out and gets us nowhere and merely keeps the pot of social fellowship boiling on the hob.

Do you want converts? Do you want money? Do you want candidates for the mission fields and the ministry? Do you want to make impact upon local government and eventually upon national government, upon education, trade unions, the arts? This is the way. Notice I did not ask, Do you want to build up a large congregation with a great family constantly growing in upon itself in prosperity and self-satisfaction? Because this is not the way to get a name for yourself as a 'successful' minister. For the congregation that is fed on the living Word of God and in which everything is subservient to its impact and power is a congregation which, being living, is also on the move. There will be constant comings and goings. As soon as, and sometimes even sooner than, young folk are built up in the faith, God will thrust them out here and there, far and near, at home and abroad. Others will have to take their place, and others after them, until your Church will become a clearing house and, for all but a faithful nucleus, a temporary stopping-place where men and women are charged with the Word of God before being drafted to battlefields of their own. 'There is that scattereth, and yet increaseth.' And they in different measures will reproduce their kind, and you will soon have grandchildren and great grandchildren far sooner than you could have them biologically, until they become an army.

My brothers, I believe there is more hope of this in Scotland today than for fifty, sixty, a hundred, even a hundred and twenty years. Of course there have been many movements back to the Word of God, both sound and spurious, and there have been many movements back to the Spirit of God both resoundingly loud-mouthed and spurious. The one without the other, the Word without the Spirit, or the Spirit without the Word, is useless. But bring the two together: no mere sound orthodoxy, sound asleep or stone dead, and no mere pentecostal ecstasy flying kites high in the wind of but a few scattered, hag-ridden texts, but the 'Word of God which liveth and abideth for ever' in its fulness, having become in God's man crucified flesh, pouring itself forth from anointed lips in burning consecrated power, and we may yet see in our beloved land a movement which will make the 'Fifty-Nine revival look pale, and which may bring in a day of sober revival and intoxicated persecution to make the angels in heaven marvel, and the Father-heart of

God rejoice for the sufferings of His Son, and the glory of His Name.

Yours sincerely,
WILLIAM STILL

22/SPECIAL MISSIONS

May 1964

My Dear Friends,

I want to write about special missions.[1]

The first city-wide mission I had experience of was that of Lionel Fletcher when as a youth I learned of the profound impacts made upon city ministers, notably J. S. Stewart, then of Beechgrove, the late Victor Caldwell of West St. Clement's, and the late Gilbert Gordon of St. Paul's. These impacts reverberated, I remember, through the respective congregations. I have no doubt that the deep impression made upon Professor Stewart then has something to do with his almost apostolic utterances, especially on prayer, made during this his moderatorial year.

Within a year of my coming to Gilcomston, Billy Graham came to Aberdeen with the Youth for Christ team from America and, preaching powerfully in Gilcomston, established the beginnings of Youth for Christ here before he left the city. That same year (1946) came Alan Redpath and Geoffrey Lester in a fruitful campaign, but which was the occasion (nothing to do with these men) of serious disruption of the Evangelistic Association which robbed it of most of

[1] A united evangelistic mission was taking place in 1964, of which William Still later wrote, 'From time to time these missions were arranged and a pistol was virtually placed at our heads to co-operate or else be regarded as anti-evangelical. We learned not to fall for this, although we suffered opprobrium for it.'

its Church of Scotland representation and support. Then in 1955 came Billy Graham again (by then a world-famous evangelist) to Kelvin Hall, to Aberdeen by relays, and in person. I was in charge of counselling. I have therefore had some experience of large missions, with particular opportunities for assessing their fruits, initial and eventual.

But I have since had experience of something else; namely, the systematic preaching of the whole Word of God, in one place, and over a good many years. I have seen the fruit of that, too, although I am, like others, an unprofitable servant of God. I have two things to say now. The first is that God called me to this, not that: the second is that it appears to me that 'that' ('evangelisticism') is not as good a way of evangelizing as 'this' (the fruitful witness of the members of Christ's Church built up in their faith and scattered throughout the community and the world). It is not, of course, for me to criticize or gainsay men who have been called to evangelize in that way. God has not called me to that, but out of it; I must not, therefore, abandon my God-given task (neither the hours of the week nor my powers are sufficient to do it as I would) to engage in another arduous task. And since I see the one task as more biblical and apostolic than the other, I can only express my refusal in Nehemiah's words: 'I am doing a great work, so that I cannot come down: why should the work cease, whilst I leave it, and come down to you?'

But there is more to be said. A teaching ministry is very costly, and, unhappily, the most painful part of its cost is the strange dissociation of evangelistic folk from it, as if it were a worse sin to concentrate on Bible teaching than to become Romish, or liberal, or even morally reprehensible. To be led along this road is to encounter greater ostracism than upon any other; and whereas we soon get used to the contempt, antipathy, and misrepresentation of worldly society and anti-evangelical interests, the bitterness of evangelistic animosity to a teaching ministry is something very hard to understand and account for. The only reasonable explanation I can find is that which I first 'hit' upon when we turned from evangelism to teaching. We discovered that evangelistic folk who sat so benignly under the preaching of justification by faith became quite fiendishly incensed when the Word was turned upon them unto sanctification. This, we fear, involves a truth as deep as it is significant, and ominous; and still obtains.

Now, if we were against evangelism, it is plain that the Word of God stands against us, and we have not got a leg to stand upon. But then, *we* should know that better than most, for it is *we* who have preached through and commented upon the whole Bible repeatedly! Do we twist the truth? Are we all deceived? (Happy the 'deception' that has sent so many fruitful servants of God into the world!). But this does not give us warrant for saying that all who engage in 'evangelisticism' have a vested interest in warding off the sharp point of the Word of God from their own hearts and consciences. But until we see some evidence that ardent advocates of special missions are bearing fruitful witness in their normal lives and service, and that they are engaged in sowing and watering the Word of God in the hearts of the people (as distinct from dispensing mere Gospel texts and clichés), and that, consequently, grand campaigns are organized, not as diversions from the monotony of evangelistic routine, or to cover up fruitlessness and failure in normal witness, but to reap the harvest of a sowing time, we must resolutely refuse to be distracted from our own fruitful work.

Our answer to those who condemn us (and who are they to condemn us? Romans 14:4) for our refusal to give special efforts precedence over our own work is this: If you are called of God to that kind of work, then you have a right to our sympathy and prayers (albeit we cannot look at your work, any more than our own, uncritically). But, then, we have a right to your sympathy and prayers for our work also, and that is certainly not what Gilcomston has received from the generality of evangelistic folk these last two decades. And as you are not likely to abandon your work to share in ours (why should you?), neither should you expect us, we hope, to abandon ours to share in yours. We should each thank God that the other is doing a piece of work that we are not doing. This is the attitude which should prevail between complementary parts of the Lord's work, and we have found it possible and right to have active sympathy and to pray for pieces of Christian work very different from our own that would, we believe, never be part of our calling. And all 'that there should be no schism in the body'. But does this attitude prevail? We are not saying we are guiltless or faultless. Sometimes the loneliness of our furrow tempts us to self-pitying and recriminatory thoughts; but we do try to give active support to evangelistic work by our prayers as well as by the co-operation of our individual members as they choose. If we had a like spirit of prayer and sympathetic interest from the evangelical constituency around us we do not think we would hear the unkind and cutting things that, unfortunately, do reach our ears, sooner or later.

After all, for a work which has been declared to be dying since the beginning of 1947 (when Saturday Prayer and Daily Bible Reading Notes began) there has been a remarkable run of fruit—far more than we have statistical account for, although what we could list (God forbid!) would make an astonishing record. But we must not mention it. 'Ssssssh!' they say: 'this is pride and conceit. Lie down and die.' But, No; except in the sense that we must go on dying to the slights of men in order that the work may continue and increase in fruit-bearing. Let *them* lie down and die, in this fruitful sense, and one of the first fruits of that dying would be to thank God with fervent hearts that there was a Gilcomston and for what God has done there. We have watched for nineteen years the attempts of many ardent Christians with various evangelical associations of one kind or another, including ourselves, to quicken this piece of work and that in our area, without much success; and we could have told them all, and do so, now, that there is no hope of any such piece of work being blessed which despises Gilcomston, for God has made it a light in this part of the country—not to say beyond—and He will not let His work be slighted with impunity.

What about a little of this sort of dying amongst evangelistic folk for a change? Is it not shocking that people who make such vocal witness should be in the main so frantically unwilling to suffer the Word that slays (Heb. 4:11–13), and then peevishly envy its fruits in transformed lives? This is to refuse the death and resurrection of Jesus Christ in the only practical sense. It is one thing to subscribe to the historic fact and doctrine (you don't need to be evangelistic to do that); but another to let that death challenge our life. Paul was determined to fill up whatever was lacking of the afflictions of Christ in his flesh for the Church's sake. And it is this death the Christian family must ever be dying, that life may be born in others (2 Cor. 4:10–12).

What is this, if not the only ground and possibility of fruitful evangelism?—and with no public flourish of trumpets, but that of lives eventually transformed.

Yours sincerely,

WILLIAM STILL

23/CHILDREN AND THE CHURCH (2)

September 1966

My Dear Friends,

We have had an interesting summer at Gilcomston. There have been many visitors, and the shorter services and children's addresses have encouraged parents to bring their children to Church, in the evening as well as in the morning.

This suggests that it may not be inappropriate to say a word about the training of children in respect of Church attendance. It should be clear that if we are to lead our children into godly ways we have to ignore many modern precepts and emphases. The idea that children should have a say in whether they go to Church or not is as ridiculous as to suggest that they should have a say in whether they should go to bed or not, or to school or not; for Church is at least as important. Or do you disagree? The idea that children should be masters of their life before they understand what is important for them, is against both reason and sound psychology. Children do not want such responsibility thrust upon them, and if they do seem to want it, the discontent it breeds and the difficulties it creates for them should be proof enough to discerning parents, guardians, and teachers, that they are not yet fit to choose wisely for themselves.

This, even in our congregation, may raise a protest against children sitting so long and so much in Church. Well, the services are shorter now, but is it possible that it is parents who themselves tend to be unhappy under the ministry who do not bring their children to Church? It is astonishing how many parents fear lest their children become what they call 'too religious'. They do not want them to be bad, but they do not want them to be too good, either! This is a dangerous attitude, and the only escape from its dangers is to become themselves 'very religious', by which we mean, give themselves wholly to Christ.

Certainly the difficulties of keeping children in reasonable behaviour in Church are sometimes exaggerated. During the summer we have had all but infants sitting in Church, morning and evening, and I have not been distracted even slightly by them. This is not to say that some in the pews have not been distracted by little ones fidgeting, but if parents can keep their children in reasonable behaviour by discreetly giving them suitable reading or writing material, or some other seemly occupation, then the problem is somewhat solved. The rejoinder to this may be that there is no sense in taking children to Church unless to attend to what is being said and done. But no one expects children to attend to a whole adult service: if they get something from the children's address and their own hymn, and sit for the rest in the atmosphere of worship, that is all that can reasonably be expected at first, and surely that is something. In spite of the difficulties it is a question of whether our love for our children is of the order of Christ's, who is more concerned about them coming to Him than about anything else in life, or whether it is of an order which wants to pander to them in everything, and ends up by ruining them.

These remarks may upset some. But we have the example of a number of children, mostly under ten, who have been sitting through the evening service week-by-week, and we have no evidence that they are becoming warped creatures; the very reverse in fact, they are among the happiest children we know. Not only so, but some of them, in spite of their little antics and the cost in distraction to others, can gather enough from the service to surprise their parents.

Children from an orphan home had been coming to the evening service for some months and were then forbidden to come. The sorrow of these children, and the pathetic notes they have written to the minister about their loss—not least the loss of friends they made at our Church—wring the heart. God forbid that our children should grow up with less desire for God's house, and for all that may be found within it!

Yours sincerely,
WILLIAM STILL

24/THE PATTERN OF THE MINISTRY

June 1967

My Dear Friends,

It was not untimely that our recent Congregational Mission followed hard on the heels of 1966, a year of general reappraisal of our work.[1] The Mission genuinely, and in some cases deeply, stirred hearts, both of those visiting and of those visited, and the six sermons have increased the conviction that more emphasis on proclamation is still needed in the ministry of the Word. This cannot be done by mere resolve, much less by trick or technique, but must

[1] The congregation participated in the Church of Scotland Parish Development Programme which consisted of two visitations of the parish and congregation and a series of special sermons. This came at a point in the preaching ministry when the sermons at the evening services in particular were shortened and directed specifically to those who were not yet Christians. On many occasions the evening service would be one hour shorter, so that the new emphasis could not fail to be noticed.

come from God. We believe—*I* believe, at any rate—that God is with us in this, and will help us. For the teaching of the Word which, watered by many prayers, is fruitful, must not diminish, yet must enunciate the Gospel clearly, and with Spirit-born power and thrust.

We have been saying that in two decades the Lord has taken us full circle from a narrowly aggressive evangelistic ministry through one of systematic Bible teaching back to a re-emphasis on proclamation; but someone not unacquainted with dialectical philosophy says that it has not been a cycle, but a spiral. So be it!

This transition will be misunderstood, as was the change in 1947, and some will think that change admits error. Not necessarily! Hear people arguing about the relative merits of Spring and Autumn, the current season usually winning; but what we have to learn is that Spring, and Autumn—even Winter if you know how to apply the figure—must be simultaneous. Surely it stands to reason that a long ministry cannot be sustained without ringing many changes and going through many permutations. The Holy Spirit is not static, but on-going, and therefore those who follow Him must be ready, within principles, to change also.

Some have commented favourably on the change in preaching, but we must not make odious comparisons. It must not be either/or, but both together. If we learn this, it will be a greater achievement than establishing one emphasis or another separately.

Our present position has been wrought out laboriously in agonies of corporate and private prayer, and we now see that other factors are involved than those we have had in mind. One of them is that, despite being on the eve of a great mission, many evangelistic folk in our area are depressed about that sort of work, and some are still casting aspersions upon us for 'abandoning' that kind of ministry in 1947 in which, they say, we ought still to be giving a lead. The answer is, our years of Bible-teaching ministry, and its manifest although uncomputed—and, alas, unadmitted—statistics. People who cannot see them, cannot be trusted to see anything truly.

Yet it astonishes us that there should be this lament, because we have always thought by the announcements of individual projects and efforts of a more united order that there was a measure of active and aggressive evangelism going on. True, many of these have petered out, and some should have been allowed to do so when they ceased to be effective; but has it all been so unfruitful? People say so.

If that is true, is it not a word from God to evangelistic people that they need to know the Bibles they profess to believe and which they have refused to know when its sword has been pointed at their hearts rather than at the hearts of the unconverted? How could God bless the efforts of those who have reproached and despised our years of Bible-teaching ministry which has never been without fruit, either of conversions or richer fruit, or both!

God is speaking to those who would win souls for Christ, saying that fruitful evangelism must be rooted in the ministry of the whole Word, so that those won may understand that they are committed to nothing less than the building of Christian character and the service of Christ. Then the whole life—not an artificially organized part of it—becomes a witness, and its aim is unaffected friendship with the unconverted for Christ's sake, which may lead us into strange places and situations and often expose us to bitter reactions. The other pole of that life is the aim to bring those befriended to the teaching and preaching of the saving Word, with the warfare of the prayer room as the impetus and direction behind both.

Let us state this again. The two poles of the fruitful

Christian life are, friendship with the unconverted for Christ's sake, and bringing them at the judicious, God-guided moment under the sound of the saving Word in the community and fellowship of the local Church. The needy are then drawn to Christ in the context of two norms, that of unfeigned friendship with them for Christ's sake in the world, and that of hearing Christ speak to them through His Word in the Church.

Yours to this end,
WILLIAM STILL

25/TRIBUTE TO A MOTHER

November 1967

My Dear Friends,

The passing of my mother has been more than a family event, as was evident from the congregation which gathered for the funeral service.[1] Beyond the family and its branches, there was a large representation of the Gilcomston fellowship, and some of our associated fellowships were also represented by their ministers, our own young men. Among many others there was a goodly number of Salvationists.

Our mother, at the age of eighty-eight, had bravely accepted the risks of major surgery, and survived it wonderfully, but took a turn for the worse, after which her condition steadily declined. She loved life, even with the burden of advancing years, but she was often weary by reason of increasing infirmities. Since she had a better Home, for all the love she was surrounded with down here, it would have been wrong to grudge her her rest, however much we

[1] Mrs Helen Still died on 25 October, 1967.

mourned our irreparable earthly loss. Indeed, the days before her passing were fraught with such sweet sorrow that her room was often like the gate of heaven. Even when she was beyond halting attempts to sing the songs of Zion (songs which obviously enraptured her soul with new meaning as she approached the threshold of heaven) the beatific smile was a manifest token that she was already half-way to the fields of glory, and to the sight of that Face which had shone through the gloom of many of her dark, earthly days.

Our mother had had a hard life, not because fisher-folk worked harder in those days than anyone does today, but because clouds early shadowed her adult life, although not before the grace of God lighted on her at the age of seventeen. Whatever degree of choice she had as a girl, it is clear that she desired above all else to serve Christ and, if possible, on some mission field. It was not to be, and this, I believe, was the sorrow which underlay all other sorrows of her life. I am in no doubt about this, for when I eventually found myself in the Lord's service, (I had earlier attempted to enter it, but was frustrated by ill-health, which was a grief to her) she confided that that was what she had wanted to do with her life, and it was her prayer therefore that God would choose at least one of her bairns. She could hardly have expected it to be myself, since I was the sickly one of the family, and was thought of kindly but rather hopelessly as not likely to be fit for any career. But her sympathy saved me, along with the knowledge that God does sometimes choose the weak.

This, then, was the secret heart and mind of the woman who was our mother, and, although none of this was known to us (possibly my elder brother and sister knew more than I did) the radiance of her life, often half-hidden in mists of tears and punctuated by unexplained sighs, was known to us; and we often saw her about her household tasks with tears in her eyes, but always with a song of unwavering faith in the Lord on her lips. Seemliness, and consideration for the feelings of my brothers and sisters and our many cousins, forbids me to tell of the things this courageous and tenacious woman endured in her long life, although I do think that sometime in some way her story should be recorded to the glory of God and in tribute to her indomitable faith. Perhaps the hardest thing was that she was such a tender-hearted, sensitive soul, who loved being loved almost as well as she loved loving. How she fought and slaved, scraped and sacrificed for us could perhaps never be told adequately, but it can be explained: it was by the grace of God.

Yet our mother was essentially a simple woman, with a minimal formal education, as was the way in those days. Yet her family, like that of our father from the same village of Gardenstown, was of good standing, highly respected in the community, and was known for its wholehearted evangelical interest, the measure of prosperity it enjoyed which came from hard work, and for its intellectual and artistic interests, not very common among fisher folk in those days. But there was no time for such things when hungry, needy bairns were around, so that it was not until the evening of our mother's days that she had leisure to read, and indulge her love of the lady-like arts. In recent years we often had fun when we came on her with her books—several translations of the Scriptures and the Daily Bible Reading Notes—seeking earnestly to understand some knotty point. Yet she was never pretentious about what we teasingly called her 'studies'. It was simply a thirst for spiritual knowledge that drew her on.

This leads me to note the great burden of our mother's later years as I knew her: her desire for holiness, to be right with God, and to be pleasing to Him, and her fervent prayers that her family might follow her in this. If anyone let the Word of God search the heart, she did. What a tender conscience she had about sin! Listening to the tape-recordings of the Gilcomston services became her weekly worship, and woe betide us if we showed less than the greatest reverence while she listened.

Another great burden of her heart was the Lord's work in and through our church, and I doubt if we will ever know down here what we owe to her prayers. I am wistful when I think how many of them are yet to be answered. How much they know, where she has gone, we do not know (it is surely more than we know down here); but if they do know what is taking place on earth (Moses and Elijah could not have been ignorant when they came to discuss current events with Jesus on the mount), what pleasure our mother will yet have in heaven from the answers to her oft anguished prayers!

Recently our eldest sister, with a pride which astonished me (because we are not a demonstrative family), said 'I have known many great and godly Salvation Army officers, many of them of the highest ranks; but I have never known anyone as fearless in their Christian witness as she. It did not matter who it was, she was proud of her Saviour in any company, and would rather embarrass men—and did—than allow the Lord's name to be held in disrepute, or ignored.'

But it is as a mother that we her children think of her most of all. What tender sympathy, what heart and tears of compassion for us in our sorrows and disappointments, what angry care when any would do us harm! And her justness with us all! As we were all different (who knew better than she?), we were also all alike to her. And I think it was that motherly justice, and the respect it inculcated in us for one another, which has kept us and will, I believe, keep us firmly bound together.

A word about the funeral service: With Gordon Ross at the organ (he postponed a much-needed holiday to be there) and the readings and prayers of James and George Philip, it was a memorable occasion. The dignity and sweetness, the holy hush and haunting strains of much-loved hymns, the wealth and weight of exquisitely chosen words, were unforgettable. Surely lasting good was done that day, which would please our mother most of all. So we leave her with the Lord, which is far better.

I would like to add a word about my sister Barbara, who has been a faithful Salvationist for almost fifty years. She and my elder brother John not only bore the brunt of the family's early fiery trials, but in the evening of our parents' days, it was she who bore the burden of caring for them and attending to their needs. This she has done with sacrificial devotion for which the rest of us owe her an incalculable debt. The promise attached to the fifth commandment, of long life to those who honour their parents, ought to be fulfilled particularly to her. God give her peace, satisfaction, and joyous expectation, with us all, of a full reunion in the presence of the Saviour!

May we as a family express through these pages our profound gratitude for all the loving kindness and tender sympathy shown to us at this time, and give praise to God for all the powerful upholding we have been conscious of in our time of need.

Yours very sincerely,
WILLIAM STILL

26/JESUS AND THE SAMARITAN WOMAN

March 1970

Dear Friends,

I want to write about out attitude to Christian vocation and service. A thing one sees with increasing clarity in an enlivening church is that beyond the basic vocation of each—housewife, electrician, nurse, lecturer, or business woman—there is specifically Christian service to be rendered which each may find if he or she will, and fulfil, if prepared to co-operate with others.

But we must do some hard thinking about the relation between the two, lest, on the one hand, we see our vocation simply as our job in life, just as unbelievers do: or, on the other hand, see our Christian service as merely providing some skill to help the organization of the church to function.

The answer to both problems is the same, namely, doing everything, yes, *everything*, in, with, and for, Jesus Christ. Nor is this to be done detachedly, as practising a piece of exalted Christian philosophy—'This is the right thing to do'—and often doing it without imagination or romance, but doing it in the realization of holy, intimate and homely fellowship, with Christ, as the present, practical, and immediate Guide of our life.

I was talking to a group about this in the context of one of my favourite encounters, that of Christ with the woman of Samaria. I was pointing out that the reason why Jesus approached the woman at the well so naturally was that the issue of the encounter was already in His Father's hands. To put it otherwise and more strikingly, it was because Jesus had cast all the burden of His service upon His Father that He approached the well and the woman without a care in the world, and knew precisely what He should do and say. There is a sense in which Jesus had no will of His own. His will was His Father's. And that is our cue.

But, you may say, He had cares. His immediate cares were tiredness, thirst, hunger, and probably in that order. He was 'a mere Man', and perhaps never so much as in this incident. But He did not throw His religion overboard. He placed it under the sovereign, perfect care of His heavenly Father. It was therefore with complete detachment from the self-conscious higher aims of hunting souls that He approached the woman.

Of course we can exaggerate the detachment, and probably need to do so to shock people. For Jesus knew where He was going. 'He had to pass through Samaria' (Jn. 4:4), which doubtless means that that was the normal way to Galilee (there were other ways). I could believe that, as Jesus saw the woman coming, He was so relaxed from 'higher' considerations that He didn't even think of sending a sky-telegram to His Father for help! Perhaps His highest conscious thought was, 'Ah, she's got a pitcher. I'll get a drink'. Not that He ignored the woman in seeking service from her. He could never do that. But He was as unself-conscious of her as a perfect Gentleman could be.

There was certainly nothing strained or tense or scheming in His manner. There did not need to be, for His dependence upon His heavenly Father was complete and absolutely steady. He counted on Him, and it may well be that throughout His life He frequently prayed to His Father not so much because He needed to, but because He wanted to. A lover does not need to write or telephone his beloved as often as he does. He certainly wants to. But even if he cannot, the understanding abides and the trust is unshaken, whatever happens. At least that is so with some people. How much more with Jesus and His Father!

So He went ahead as a tired, thirsty and hungry Man, and having found a ledge of the well to sit on, and a woman carrying a pitcher to draw water with, He began conversation by asking for a drink. Now, for a godly man to begin a conversation by asking, or offering, a drink is really very worldly, especially since it is not always water people drink! But it was she, not He, who quibbled. In her eyes He was the superior Jew, but it was she who objected to the freedom of His behaviour. As she approached, she may have had the common Samaritan chip-on-the-shoulder about the Jews. That made her difficult. People with chips-on-the-shoulder do make life difficult for others, and it is often hard to be natural with them. Sometimes, in the matter of anything as simple as asking for, or giving a drink, they raise all sorts of political, religious, and moral questions—the sort of questions that keep people apart and keep them from helping one another and enjoying fellowship with one another. That is a pity, for some of the best and most lasting friendships have begun by a sudden impulse of friendship from one stranger to another, perhaps in a crowd, an impulse which was not repulsed.

But someone may say, Are you not relegating politics, religion, and morals to rather an unimportant place in life? Not necessarily; but these are the things which do hinder communications between people, are they not? What kept the Jews and Gentiles apart in the apostle Paul's day but these barriers which the great little man wrought so hard to demolish! For the most important thing in the world is contact between personalities, quite apart from politics, religion, and morals.

The Man wanted a drink: let Him have it—and quick,

woman! The noontide sun is beating down on His burning head! But she didn't hurry. She must quibble first, and did so. He never got His drink. Of course He forgot about it, as He forgot about His hunger and His tiredness also, when He saw that there was work to do. But it was only because the dear Man was able to be a mere human being, when there was nothing else to be, that He could show His divine identity when there was no need to do so. The two go together, the humanity and the divinity. And the one is never far from the other, however the connection may seem to be hidden for a time. For the faith that is prepared to leave all to God when that is what is needed, is also the faith that is prepared to draw upon God when that is needed. Even then, it still does so unselfconsciously, in preoccupying involvement, as Jesus with this woman's salvation.

Am I off my subject? No: I am right on it. *We need to live like Jesus.* That we cannot do so perfectly down here is no reason why we ought not to do so with all our might—or should I say with all God's might. What I am trying to say is that what was on our Lord's mind as He came to the well was His tiredness, thirst and hunger, rather than the woman and her salvation. Not that He did not care for the woman or her salvation—that was what He came to earth for—but He could, sometimes, be a private Man and care for Himself. I believe it was the pitcher as much as the woman that He saw.

I am sure that some of you reading this may think that I am making out our Lord to be carnal. I am also sure that if you are, it is because you have got your ideas of what is carnal mixed up. 'You are too religious!' said Paul to the Athenians. We also are, in the wrong sort of way.

But what has this got to do with vocation and service? Everything! For our problem is that we can't be natural! Everything we do is tainted with unnaturalness because we don't believe God can bless that sort of thing. But that is exactly what He does bless. For one thing, it is real. We *are* natural. How can God bless us when trying to be what we are not? You know—holy wraiths, walking as if by levitation several feet above the ground! We are so religious. It is not natural! But Jesus is natural, because He has complete faith in the hugeness of His Father's love, and power to add the supernatural dimension to life when and where it is needed. If you like, you can say He was natural because He was spiritual; and that is true, although I don't want to make too much of a concession to that argument at the moment.

You may not like the picture of Jesus as a mere Man hurrying His last dragging footsteps to the well and thinking only of His tiredness, hunger and thirst; but you like the picture of His magnificent dealings with the needy woman. Well, I say, the two—my picture and yours—belong together. I also say that you may never know the second experience yourself in a like encounter until you know the humanness of the first. 'You are too religious!'

But the most important thing has yet to be said. If Jesus was hurrying slowly to that well, longing for a drink and rest and food like any ordinary man, He was doing so in company with His Father. As He went He was saying, 'Oh Father, I am tired and thirsty and hungry.' And if His Father had said to Him, 'Son, you have a woman to save before you get a drink,' then, of course, when the time came and the opportunity was at hand, He forgot His thirst entirely (see Jn. 4:32). But it was the naturalness of His companionship with His Father that made the transition from natural to spiritual so effortless.

So with us. When we are preaching, or printing, or scrubbing, or making tea at church and something goes wrong, we ought to say 'Oh, Father!' or 'Oh, Lord!' The same at home, and at work, or on holiday, or wherever and whenever. The soul that is in that state of intimacy with its God and Saviour is ready for higher service.

One last word: if you think I paint Jesus as too natural, and therefore ourselves also by association with Him, remember that apart from our own private religious life, which is no one's business but God's and our own, there is a life which some of us live, with thirty to fifty others, two-and-a-half hours per week, and at other times, too, in prayer. So perhaps we have some right to say these things. What does religiosity hide? Have a look at Matthew 23:1–12!

Yours sincerely,
WILLIAM STILL

27/GOD'S WORD A HAMMER!

April 1970

Dear Friends,

Listen to what God says through Jeremiah 23:23–32:

'Am I a God at hand, says the Lord, and not a God afar off? [24]Can a man hide himself in secret places so that I cannot see him? says the Lord. Do not I fill heaven and earth? says the Lord. [25]I have heard what the prophets have said who prophesy lies in my name, saying, I have dreamed, I have dreamed! [26]How long shall there be lies in the heart of the prophets who prophesy lies, and who prophesy the deceit of their own heart, [27]who think to make my people forget my name by their dreams which they tell one another, even as their fathers forgot my name for Baal? [28]Let the prophet who has a dream tell the dream, but let him who has my word speak my word faithfully. What has straw in common with wheat? says the Lord. [29]Is not my word like fire, says the Lord, and like a hammer which breaks the rock in pieces?[30]Therefore, behold I am against the prophets, says the Lord, who steal my words from one another. [31]Behold, I am against the prophets, says the Lord, who use their tongues and say, 'Says the Lord.' [32]Behold, I am against those who prophesy lying dreams, says the Lord, and who tell them and lead my people astray by their lies and their recklessness, when I did not send them or charge them; so they did not profit this people at all, says the Lord.

Now, pick out verses 28, 29. There are lots of people in the Lord's service who do not *have* His Word. There are various reasons why they do not have it, but we are not going into that now. Suffice it to say that many do not have it, and therefore cannot give it to others.

But there are many in the Lord's service who do have the Lord's Word, yet for one reason or another, known to themselves, do not speak it faithfully. They are either not prepared in the first place to let the Word hurt them, or are then not prepared to let it hurt other people; and so they cushion, pad, and muffle their failures to do so with various excuses.

I constantly hear of situations in Christ's church in various parts of the country and the world which need some kind of drastic action or another, to deal with irregularities, anomalies, corrupt or bitter or demonic behaviour. All the time God's workmen have His hammer in their hands to smash these evils in pieces, and yet seem to turn His hammer into india-rubber. They then turn round and wail and lament, and even seek to extricate themselves from situations with which they have refused to deal in the only way they can be dealt with. The blind refusal of the Lord's servants to see this is one of the most amazing things. They are so blind that when it is suggested that what this situation, and that, requires is the authoritative Word of God, they will say, 'Yes, we really ought to have a Bible study, but so few will come to one during the week.' If you ask, 'But what do you do on Sundays when you meet in church?', they say, 'I preach.' 'Well, what do you preach?' 'I preach the Word of God' 'Yes, but how do you preach it? Do you find the place and the passages, and address yourself to the local situation in plain terms, to bring the evils, there present, into the open?' The answer is generally, 'O you can't do that! You would have the place about your ears; people would not stand for it. You can't do that!' But do you not see that by taking this view, you have tied yourself, hands and feet, and have shut your own mouth for fear of people who desperately need God's Word on certain issues, and you will not give it to them?

Do you not see the devil's strategy in this? There is not a situation in Christ's church in the whole wide world that cannot be dealt with by the Word of God. There is nothing else to deal with it. What other authority or means have we for dealing with evils but God's Word? That Word, if we ransack it from cover to cover, has the very word for our situation. I am amazed at the ineptitude not only of individuals, but of whole schools of thought, and even denominations, in respect of evils which beset and bedevil their work. I have been saying to some for years that the way to deal with the evil of certain secret societies which have sapped the vitals of Christian denominations for years with their subtle, but really ridiculous evils, is to bring them out into the open. What the Christian church needs in so many situations is great rows! The Holy Spirit in the Acts of the Apostles is not afraid of disturbance. Sometimes it is necessary.

I know that that will shock many, and they will dismiss what I am saying out of hand because it appears to them blatantly unchristian. I have seen many causes of strife which cannot be dealt with but by prayer; but major evils, radical departures from biblical orthodoxy, deep corruption, bitter feuds, and adamant worldliness may not be dealt with by prayer without action. Trace the course of our Lord's three years' ministry and you will see that in the end He brought everything out into the open, the climax of which is seen in the Gospel according to Matthew from chapter 21 onwards, especially chapters 23 and 24. If anyone ever used the Word of God as a hammer to break the rock in pieces, or as wildfire to set the straw, or as we say in Scotland, the heather on fire, it was Jesus. 'Gentle Jesus, meek and mild.' Yes, sometimes, and thank God for it (see Is. 42:1–4). But not always. Other situations call for other treatment.

Mind you, this kind of action calls for extreme selflessness and crucifixion. I have waited months before bringing a vexed situation into the open, not so much because the situation was not ripe for it, but because I was not fit to deal with it in love. All natural animosity, bitterness, frustration, has to be weaned from the heart before one can tackle such a situation in a spirit that God will own, and use, unto its own solution or correction. And the very fact of lying low and seeming for a time not to care gives sinners a false sense of security and really prepares them for the maximum impact of the Word suddenly unleashed upon them, to their folding-up, or getting themselves into a paroxysm of rage, which makes the enormity of their sin clear to all, even perhaps to themselves.

I wish this plain word could be circulated wherever Christ's church runs into internal difficulties, because I am convinced that it is a major strategy of the devil in our day (but doubtless nothing new) to blind the most sensible people to the fact that the remedy for their plight is in their hands. Take a New Testament word from Ephesians 6;17,

18: 'And take . . . the sword of the Spirit, which is the Word of God. Pray . . . in the Spirit, with all prayer. . . .'

Yours sincerely,
WILLIAM STILL

28/AN APPEAL TO BACKSLIDERS

May 1970

Dear Friends,

When I was lamenting the other day that too many middle-aged folk who have been in Gilcomston for twenty years and more have settled down to a comfortable life and opted out of the Christian battle, the remark was made, 'Perhaps they haven't the intelligence to take it all in, and follow' Well, what do you think of that?

I must confess that I have often been tempted to think this, by way of excuse for those who have been and are a disappointment. True, a man is not much use in Gilcomston unless he applies the powers of his mind to the Word of God and tries to get a thorough grasp of the spiritual import of the Bible's history and poetry, etc. But then, I think, there are perhaps not a few of average intelligence and not much formal education who are just as much involved in the study of the Word and in the outreaches of the ministry by prayer and other effort, as, say, the academic fraternity. How is it that they can take such a hold of the truth and keep themselves so deeply involved in the multifarious activities of our congregation?

The answer is that it has nothing to do with intelligence as such, but with the will. Some have allowed their spiritual life to become dried up until the whole thing becomes a duty and then a bore, and they needs must find other outlets to make life interesting. How does it happen? It can be simply stated. Whatever the past occasion and circumstances, some have come to a place in their pilgrimage where costly obedience was called for, and they balked, and have continued to balk, until all joy and then interest in spiritual things has gone out of their lives. Now they are souls on the defensive, looking for excuses. Having found them, they are now on the look-out for substitutes for obedience, as was Saul when Samuel had to say to him, 'To obey is better than sacrifice, and to hearken than the fat of rams.'

It will not take little to shunt such lives back again on the main line of the Christian pilgrimage. But I am making another appeal, not in the interests of greater numbers attending (which some may think my motive in saying things like this, although it is known that I have been content for years with small numbers), but in the interests of the people concerned, lest they lapse into mere nominal Christianity—part of a new, dead Gilcomston which barely fulfils its minimum duty, and is just a great dead weight to be carried by an all-too-small and overworked nucleus of 'willing horses'. It is not easy, when we get into the late thirties, forties, or even fifties, and find that we have really become backsliders, to admit it, even to ourselves, let alone to others. It is much harder still to change our mode of life; but it has been done, by people with very proud streaks, and it can be done again. I am hoping that in days to come, perhaps all very quietly and without the ringing of bells, or inquisitive people taking too much notice, there will be a new returning to Bible Study and Prayer.

I know my faults, and realize the danger that meetings can go on too long. Many feel this and often appeal to me to try to keep the meetings, as well as the services, within bounds. And we are learning, slowly, although I must admit that it is hard to have one's enthusiasm for the Word and the things of God clipped because people nag about the length of meetings. Do not I also need to consider my body? But I am determined to try to keep things within bounds, time-wise, because it is often our keenest folk who are most definite that the time factor must be observed. Yet the Lord and His Word and His work are so preoccupying that it is the easiest thing in the world to forget the clock and go on and on. Would you not like to be so caught up with the movements of the Spirit working in, from, and through, our congregation that time ceased to be an overruling or dominant factor?

Anyway, what in all the world have you found to take the Lord's place? Look at it with Christian eyes, and say if you can really pit any friendship or activity or ambition or pursuit against friendship with Christ and an on-going experience of His thrilling love and marvellous companionship. Or has He faded and become so dim that you hear all that is said as from afar, where His voice is so faint that you can hardly hear the Word you used to love and live by? Is it some change in circumstances, the loss of a friend or loved one, some new turn in your way of life, a new job, a new house, or someone who has come into your life through whom you have been given a different outlook on life, that has changed your ways?

It may be that your fellow Christians have not had sufficient sympathy with you in your troubles, needs, or wants, and you don't find them as kind as some of your other friends. How long have you tested these other friends? Doubtless some Christian friends can prove fickle (is this not what we find in the Lord's service, alas?). But you must remember that some of us have been together for a very long time, and our friendship for one another has stood the test of a quarter of a century, and there is a depth of care for one another at Gilcomston that you will not find in many places, in or out of Kirk, today. Ought you not to be part of it? There are not a few to whom the fellowship of Christian service means more than association with non-Christian flesh and blood. For them it is often a relief to get away from those who have no time for Christ, in order to savour again the depths of trust, love, and understanding that can only be found among folk bound together in the closest and strongest of bonds, namely, common love to Christ and devotion to His service.

I am sure that there are quite a few on the fringe of our congregation who think they do pretty well by way of attendance, because of other duties and, it may be because of certain delicacy of health, etc., etc., but who could give themselves to the Lord and His work in Gilcomston without any injury to health and other legitimate interests if they could just find the enthusiasm they once had for the things of God. Are you more thrilled by a visit to the theatre, or to the house of a friend, or by an outing, than by a visit to the Lord's house? Then you have lost something, if you ever had it, which can change the colour and trend of your whole life and give new zest to every other legitimate thing. Who are those who appreciate the natural gifts of God most? Those who appreciate *Him* most.

What about it? Am I the cause of your stumbling? Then what about asking to have a word with me, and tell me about it? Do not be afraid. I won't take offence, or turn on you. If I have done you wrong, or failed you, I am ready to express the deepest regret and make what amends I can; only do not let that keep you from finding out what you need in Christ and in Christian fellowship. I plead with you to listen, as with all the mellowness of the love Christ has given me for people over the years, I ask you to make up your mind that you are going to change. I do not want you to make a fuss about this. The quietest and least obtrusive approach is the best. Ease yourself in gently. There are always a few, alas, who will want to make your change of habit a 'speak'; horrid creatures, so give them as little to say or think as possible. Perhaps you can best reinstate yourselves through some trusted friend in whom you can confide. Think about it, and pray about it, and God will tell you what to do.

Yours very kindly,
WILLIAM STILL

29/CHILDREN AND THE CHURCH (3)

June 1970

Dear Friends,

Although I declined our Kirk Session's very kind offer to mark my twenty-five years of ministry in Gilcomston and they accepted this with astonishing good humour, I must mention it, as we approach and pass that anniversary of my induction (which took place on 7th June, 1945). I do not know how well I may succeed in what I want to say, or how far it may be understood, but I hope and pray that I may succeed and you may understand.

It is the simplest things that are most difficult to understand and accept, and one of those which seems in my experience to have been most difficult for people to understand and accept has been the fact that the Lord demands of His servants, each and every one of them, to listen to Him only and obey His will implicitly, irrespective of what it costs. There have been times in the stages of our progress through the years when the pattern of congregational life seems to have become set, when there was a general assumption that this was 'it'—for evermore, or, at least, for the duration of that generation. Then the Lord's 'cloud' moved on, and changes became inevitable, and another painful upheaval ensued. Personally I fail to see how it could be otherwise in a ministry such as mine of considerable length. No man and congregation can go on year after year, doing the same things, and keep alive unless there is, not only change, but sequence, rhythm, and (we hope) progress towards solid spiritual achievement. This must not only meet the needs of our day, but point forward, prophetically, to the spiritual needs of tomorrow and of a new generation.

This is something of which I have been deeply aware since the first revolutionary change from evangelism to teaching took place in 1946–7. God was beginning a work that would go beyond my day. That is why I have been able to conquer natural impatience, and have been able to stick to my guns through thick and thin, even when every significant group with which I might have aligned myself has disdained, or criticized what I was trying to do. This has been far from easy, for there is that within me which would naturally love to push itself to the front, and yet there is a fatal element which, I believe, renders me unfit to be a public leader. That the truth about myself and the will of the Lord have so consistently coincided, even when frustration has been exceedingly painful to the flesh, has been my greatest peace, and has kept me free from that personal ambition which could ruin what the Lord is working in our midst. God is in control, and only what He says, goes; and what He says in different days and circumstances varies considerably. This means that I, and any who are called of God to co-operate with me, must be constantly on our spiritual toes, and must be able to say daily, 'Here we have no continuing city, but we seek one to come.'

The mention of those called to co-operate with me prompts the remark that there are some who will read these words and know very well what it is to be divinely drafted into a work which has often absorbed time and energies more than they wished, and which has even kept them steadily plodding on when they wanted to make arrangements to serve the Lord elsewhere or otherwise. I am not suggesting perversity on their part, but after years of service in Gilcomston it may have been felt that new pastures were indicated—I have had this experience myself—but no! The way closes up, and it is seen that Gilcomston is still to be the sphere of their witness.

Of course, if people feel themselves to be under a mere man, that is very galling and irksome, but it only needs a little thought to see that in our congregation they are not under a man, but under God's commission, and His blessing, too. Indeed, if any sit through the services today, and do not discern the presence and power of the Spirit, then they must be spiritually insensitive, and totally lacking in response. This does not mean that the man is not to be kept in his place; he is so kept. He is not to be followed slavishly, and is certainly not to be adored, as some foolishly have sought to do. But spiritual discernment will show that up to now God has guided the fellowship through him. How, otherwise, has the work survived against so many prognostications of doom?

But this is all said preparatory to a word about changes I envisage, and which have already been heralded, more or less, from the pulpit. As to these, I believe, firstly, that real Christian worship in the nineteen-seventies will have to be less formal. I spoke recently to a Graduates' Fellowship in

Inverness about 'The Unstarching of the Church', and it is this which I feel must come, if the Holy Spirit is to have sway in our lives and in our fellowships, to draw others in, and make lasting impacts upon them. One person present at that meeting is reported to have said, 'Let go, and let God!', I suppose scathingly implying that I was advising us all merely to get rid of our inhibitions! That is far from my meaning as, I believe, that critic knows. A certain solemnity, dignity and hush befits the presence of the Holy Spirit, I am sure, but I believe that naturalness, cheerfulness, and joy are equally necessary. I also believe that the empty pomposity of Presbyterian services conducted among the generality of nominal professors of the Christian faith is a chief hindrance to these gifts of the Spirit. When the Spirit is not there, men have to do *something* to interest themselves, and this is the sort of thing they do, and then blame God for desiring it. He does not desire it.

So I want to informalise the services, gradually, and as inoffensively as possible to deeply-dyed traditional minds. We have gone a long way towards this in the evening, and all to the good, as everyone who attends will agree. (How many years—is it decades?—since you were at an evening service? How many years of Bible Study and Prayer have you ignored? God is going to ask you, one day. Is it five, ten, fifteen, twenty, or twenty-five years?). I want us to change in the morning, also, but not just in the same way as in the evening. There is infinite variety with God, and there is every reason for having the services different; but the same air of warm, dignified freedom must pervade all.

The other thing I want to do is to implement our doctrine of baptism in the bringing up of our children. It took years for me to come to an absolute conviction about covenant baptism, thanks to a variety of influences. But as the truth of our doctrine of baptism has taken hold of me, I see that it must be proved in the bringing up of our children in the Lord.

I think I began to see what was to be done through the coming of the Mackenzies with a young family.[1] There was abundant grace in that home, and discipline too; father being a paternal 'chum' to his sons and mother the maternal equivalent to her daughters. We have lived to see the young Mackenzies grow up in the fellowship to be an example to other young folk, of loyalty in attendance at all diets of worship and meetings, and of Christian witness and service in the world. Another thing that has influenced me has been the way gracious Free Church people bring up their families. Indeed, I have met not a few older folk of the United Free tradition who remember being taken to Sunday morning prayer meetings by their fathers when they were small, and even tiny. Then I am told by our brothers who have visited the wonderful Czech Christian fellowships that little children attend all their meetings, including those for Prayer and Bible Study.[2] Lastly, many in the Presbytery of Aberdeen were lately profoundly moved by the appeal of David Searle[3] who said that Sunday Schools as presently run are virtually an abdication of Christian parents' responsibility to train and bring up their own children.

I want us therefore, to transport the Sunday School into the Church, and let us have it there, as the children sit in the family pew. Nor does this exclude children whose parents do not belong to our Church: there would still be need of

[1] Andrew Mackenzie came to train for the ministry in 1960, bringing his wife and most of his family of six children.

[2] For many years the situation and needs of the Church in Czechoslovakia had been a matter of practical and prayerful concern to the Gilcomston congregation and those associated with it.

[3] Then minister of Newhills, Aberdeen, and later of The High Kirk, Larbert (where Robert Murray M'Cheyne served as assistant to John Bonar, 1835–36).

teachers or guardians to meet those, and bring them in and make them feel wanted. Some sort of informal meeting, possibly at another time, or during the week, could be arranged for them, or for all, but the basis of the whole thing would be children coming to Church and sitting with their parents and guardians. I think also that we ought to have the Primary School in Church with their parents for the first half-hour of the service. Perhaps that would relieve devoted workers of part of the almost interminable hour-and-a-half that they are expected to keep the interest of the restless tiny ones.

But all this will need to be wrought out by judicious experiment, assuming the goodwill of all, to effect change as helpfully as possible. If all accept and at least are willing to try to make it work, I feel sure we may devise patterns of Church life which will lead us into the seventies with far more success than our Kirk has had with its young folk so far this century.

One last word: don't say that children cannot do this and will not do that. Parents are sometimes too prone to say what children will do and will not do. It is not the persuasion of the children that I am concerned about, but the persuasion of the parents. A godly winner of souls said to me the other day, 'Why is it that Christian parents want their children to be less godly and more worldly than they are?' I re-echo the question, and add this to it: 'Is it because Christian parents think they have missed something by being *too* Christian?' If so, one wonders how much they have savoured the depths of the love of God in Jesus Christ. What do you think?

Yours, full of expectation,
WILLIAM STILL

30/POISE AND ITS FRUITS

January 1971

Dear Friends,

I want to discuss poise. You could call it balance, but none the less I regard poise as being as far beyond balance as a tight-rope-walker waltzing over a yawning void on a mere string is beyond a novice reaching the safe end of the rope frantically swaying within a hair's-breadth of disaster. It is the difference between a risky exploit barely accomplished, and an act of daring beautifully performed. It is the difference between mediocre accomplishment and works of skill and grace, between utility and beauty. In the realm of the spirit it represents (more than we may think or want to think) the difference between the hard labour of self-effort and riding high on the wings of Another.

In passing I would like to refer this distinction to certain areas of Christian endeavour. Take, for instance, the arduous hacking away at Scripture, compared with reading and studying the Holy Book in company with the Author and being shown the highlights of its truth as they interest and affect personal experience and enjoyment. Or think of the distinction between a solitary soul plodding his weary way through a life of toilsome righteousness without inspiration or help, and the spring in the step that faith as a gift of God, appreciated and appropriated, affords the eager contestant in the exciting race of life. Most of all I want to think of the difference between painfully muddling through one's human relationships and the gracious poise and mutual beneficence of associations in which Christian love sings its way into joyous fellowship, preserving wise restraints yet caring deeply, and opening its heart widely to share without shame or pride the common joys and sorrows of our pilgrim way.

Some folk with the best will in the world and a body of biblical knowledge just cannot manage the simplest relationships. Instead of steering their way through life with full sail and flying colours they plough through the deepest waters, plunging into troughs alternating with dizzy crests, until they never know where they are, and even who they are, in relation to other personalities. What is needed is poised control. For it is simply not possible to know who we are, let alone how we should fit in with others, unless Christ the Author and Finisher of our faith tells us. This is no imposition on His part, for He is no alien Christ, but that unique Christ who fits my soul as He fits no one else's in the whole, age-long universe. This is what the Spirit revealed when by John He promised, to those who conquer, a 'white stone' with a new name written 'which no one knows saving he who receives it.' It is a secret with Christ that none other can share. What further testimony do we need to the unique fittingness of His coming to the individual heart?

The first thing in personal relationships is to become to oneself a known and recognizable person. Where this has not been achieved by adolescence or early adulthood, it is due both to insecurity of environment and to undue sensibility to that environment. We can only know who we are in relation to others, but if those others do not help us to know who we are, the only hope is that Another may do so. Indeed only He (Christ) can enable us fully and satisfyingly to know who we really are. And when He does, we can safely emerge into any company and make at least the beginnings of relationships, for we have the first elemental orientation, namely, that we know who we are in relation to Him, our Maker, Redeemer, Saviour, and Friend. On the natural level, too, *one* human anchor is sufficient to give even the most sensitive soul a platform of self-realization, as many an orphaned, only child has proved, having a sensible, loving mother.

We need first, then, to be thirled[1] to Christ, not in theory, however knowledgeably and eloquently expressed, but in human, spiritual fellowship; knowing Christ not as a set of moral or spiritual precepts or as a verbal gospel, but as a Person, inter-penetrating and living within our personality. And yet, we are so made that the achievement of even elemental and socially preparatory self-knowledge (through the great Other) is only possible within a third polarity (!); for human life in its fulness is only possible within the triangular relationship of ourselves, Christ, and others.

For example, a soul coming to Christ in a desert island (through shreds of His Word and by the Spirit) could never grow as a fully human, Christian personality without communication with others. It is in the field of personal relationships that we come to know ourselves and that our hidden depth emerges; so that it is well that early in life we come to know ourselves through Christ, and then begin to work out who we are in relation to others.

It is here that basic balance is necessary, and then poise, not merely in a socially acceptable sense, so that we are at home with all sorts of people, but to a degree which enables us to manage our relationships realistically on a variety of different levels. Not that we begin to classify people according to what we consider their different values, for in God's sight and ours they must be accepted as of equal value; but that our personal obligation to each is different.

My duty to my mother is different in character and extent from my duty to my brother or sister. My duty to dear

[1] Thirled: in thraldom to.

friends given me by God for mutual benefit as Christian workers is different from my duty to other friends bound with me in the bundle of life but not so intimately or particularly. Then my duty to this family may be different from my duty to that, and so on, until one is able to construct, not artificially but realistically, a whole web of relationships, all different, to weave a complex and ultimately beautiful tapestry of life in which the utmost use is made of every constituent thread and colour.

One effect of this will be that we do not get into exclusive huddles which virtually ostracise others, for we will avoid yielding to the temptation of being too often together with the same people, discussing other individuals and groups, until when we meet these others the sum of all our gossip becomes a cool, distant or even hostile attitude. This, of course, is sensed at once and soon leads to factions, camps, cliques, and antipathies, to the detriment of happy relationships within the fellowship, so that harm is done to God's church and kingdom, not least in the poor witness we give to those on the fringe, sizing us up.

One thing the wise Christian will often do is review his relationships, lest thoughtless, carnal habits lead to rutted ways, and we find ourselves running in channels of actions which soon master and control us. We must remember Paul's words to the Romans, that we ought to owe no man anything but to love him. And true love is a very balanced thing. In certain cases this may involve withdrawing to some extent from this one and that in order to balance or re-balance relationships and so preserve that poise which makes life a beautiful progress into Christ, in spite of all our faults. The Holy Spirit keeps us true to Him and consequently realistically true to those with whom our earthly lot is cast. He it is who helps us to avoid certain pitfalls, so that we may not only serve our Lord better, but find greater joy in the blessings of social fellowship with loved ones and friends, not to say former enemies.

Yours sincerely to this end,
WILLIAM STILL

31/RELAX!

March 1971

My Dear Friends,

I want to write about relaxation, and I want to begin on the physical level, because the body can affect the mind as much as the mind the body. I wrote at length on this in July 1969, and I am going to repeat some of the things said there.[1] But they can bear repetition, for they are very important for health, and are said here in a different context.

My first interest in this subject was awakened as a lad of seventeen when I was introduced to the system of physical relaxation applied to pianoforte playing as devised and taught by Tobias Mathay, the teacher of Harriet Cohen, Myra Hess, and Irene Scharrer. I also learned at that time of the system of Swedish exercises taught to the Salvation Army Scouts and Guards (Guides) which was obviously much more relaxed and beautiful to watch than the tight-fisted clenching and punching movements which used to characterize their public performances before they substituted grace for brawn, as in piano-playing I learned to substitute weight for force as a means of depressing the keys.

It appears that due to mental and emotional tension of which we are largely unaware, we often impose far greater strain and tautness upon ourselves than is necessary for the calls upon our energy at a particular time. This is a simple observation, but it is astonishing how strongly human nature objects to attention being drawn to it. Recently a consultant in hospital advised a patient troubled with varicose veins to avoid altogether crossing her legs or ankles. When I shared this advice with some friends, they laughed, and I wondered whether it was the laugh of amusement or embarrassment.

But the deprecated lesson was deeper than perhaps the consultant was aware of. He was doubtless thinking primarily of the effects of physical tension on particular parts of the human anatomy; whereas I am thinking of what such physical tension represents in terms of habitual attitudes of strain to the whole personality. To one who does not adopt the practice, the habit of leaving the car in gear can be disconcerting. But why is it done? To reduce unnecessary strain and wear on the brakes. But what about our poor bodies, which are often hunched-up and tied in knots, knees or ankles gripped or locked together in a desperate, unconscious embrace as if life depended on it, when we are supposed to be in comparative repose! Some people cannot even relax in bed, and yet wonder why they cannot sleep, whereas with the simple acceptance of the fact that this prodigal waste of energy adds strain to life, and the simple determination to try to reduce it, it is possible progressively to relax the tension of our normal lives until a new kind of physical peace descends upon our bodies. It will then not be difficult for any sensible person to judge the incalculable effect this can have upon the mind and soul.

It is usual for highly-strung people to deny that they can do anything about their tension; it is the way they are made, they say. The very way that their eyes stare out of their heads proclaims that it is hard for them to relax! But even the most inveterate 'clutcher' can learn at least to reduce nervous tension (this is what in extreme cases sedative medication prescribed by the doctor is meant to do) and they might be surprised to find that what they once regarded as an emotional, or mental, or even spiritual problem, was simply a matter of learning to relax the body and letting that affect the whole personality.

Am I then implying that some of our problems in this realm may have simpler solutions than we have thought? Yes, I am, but of course I am saying it in a Christian context. Not that the same could not be said to those who do not know Christ so that the advice benefits them, but ultimately it would be necessary to unfold the whole Gospel and make it bear practically on their problem before they could hope to attain the repose which is essential to a healthy, happy, and fruitful life.

One way of putting it is simply to say that when we know God as our Saviour and Friend, with all the deliverance from care and worry that this implies (look at Heb. 2:14, 15), it is then possible to cast the whole burden of life upon Him. That is precisely what He tells us to do, so that we bear none of the burdens He died and rose again to bear for us. Instead we draw upon the resources of His gracious power to enable us to be and do what He requires of us. It is in this context only that one dares fully to advise people to learn to ease away progressively the tensions that burn up so much energy, and which make us prematurely tired and aged.

Of course, people who live busy family lives in particular will tell an old bachelor that he does not know what he is talking about! Well, I am one of six children, and I have not entirely forgotten the rough and tumble of busy family life. But that is not the point: it is such busy people, harassed with many cares, who need to learn the 'art' of relaxation much more than people who have, they may think, more opportunity to indulge it.

As I see it, it is not so much a matter of how busy one is—some people are busier than they need be—but rather of one's attitude to life, and the extent to which one lives in an atmosphere of strain which, as I say, contributes nothing to life but tiredness. To such I want to say that it is as simple in essence as this: you are not resting in the Lord. Mendelssohn's 'O, rest in the Lord' from *Elijah* is nowadays only played at funerals. I wonder why? Is it because we think that there is no possibility of resting in Him until death?

Do you know that the Epistle to the Hebrews 3:7 to 4:13 deals with the subject and problem of rest in a most wonderful way? First it applies to God resting after the creation of the universe, and then as an example of our resting in Him for salvation; the Jewish, and then the Christian sabbath being parables of that blessed rest.

We know that salvation is all of grace. Even the faith whereby we appropriate the blessing is a gift of God (Eph. 2:8). But the evil one has instilled restlessness into us because he wants us to rebel against God, as if we, like him, were so far gone in sin that no salvation was provided for us. Salvation is provided: but we can only know and enjoy it by receiving it gratuitously. Yet it takes us a whole lifetime as Christians to see that the tendency to try to work for our salvation is evilly inspired, and must be resisted at all costs. This is the ground upon which we must learn to relax our bodies, because it is ours to enjoy God. 'Man's chief end is to glorify God, and enjoy Him for ever'. The greatest, highest, and most practical truth of our life is that we are *recipients*. God has given us life, first natural, then spiritual (see 1 Cor. 15:46), and our highest duty, privilege, and pleasure is simply to acknowledge it, and enjoy it. It is the devil and the fall which have complicated what in God's eyes is completely uncomplicated. But it takes, as we have said, a whole lifetime to unlearn our bad habits, and only a thorough knowledge of the doctrines of grace will help us even to begin.

Now, I want you to begin forthwith to practise this, each according to his or her circumstances. Find the most comfortable position in a chair or couch, and consciously and deliberately relax the muscles of the body from head to feet. You may be surprised how much unsuspected tension lies within you, even when you think you are relaxing. Not only so, but you may be shocked to find that there is a whole attitude of mind which is against this process, and which can instantly think of a number of things to do at the moment, just to avoid the pain of trying to relax (see Heb. 4:11—'strive'!) I tell you, the resistance to your relaxing, even for a few, precious moments, is nothing less than a demonic plot against the health of body and soul. Resist the resistance, and hold to your attempt to relax the whole body!

Long after you think you are really relaxing, you may realize that parts of the body are not relaxing, but pushing and pressing involuntarily, and you are not committing yourself to the chair or couch at all. Or you may find that while the feet and legs are resting and not pushing, the hands are clutching, or the elbows pressing into the sides of the couch as if they had a grudge against it.

Relaxing needs practice, and a little time—God made time for our use. Persevere, and when you have learned to relax you will find that a very few moments will benefit you far more than an hour sitting gripping your body and worrying about something you cannot change. The wonderful thing is that if you succeed in relaxing the body even a little, the mind inclines to follow it, and you will very likely rise with a quieter mind, much better fitted for the strain of what lies ahead.

You will also find that the habit grows, however much you may be prone to forget. You ought also to find that even when you are not in absolute repose, you have a greater inclination to relax, even when doing some exacting task, which you will do the better on account of the absence of strain.

We know, of course, that we cannot do strenuous and skilled work with a flabby body and floppy mind: it is *controlled* relaxation that is called for, and this is what the illustration of piano-playing taught me.

Do you remember the teacher taking your hand in hers and showing you how to form letters? She might stop and say, Don't grip so hard! and you would learn from the firm gentleness of her grasp to relax also, and learn that control has to do with relaxation as much as with physical effort. Do we need to spiritualize this? Surely not!

Yours sincerely,

WILLIAM STILL

32/LIVING TO HELP THE INDIVIDUAL

January 1972

Dear Friends,

I want to write about caring for people. I do so with trepidation since my busy life precludes caring for people as I ought and they need. None-the-less, even to my own condemnation I must air the subject because of the challenge it presents, especially to readers who are intent on becoming caring Christians.

I need not enumerate my own burdens, since those interested in the work understand most of them. There is certainly a growing reservoir of willing help in the work, not least in prayer, which makes it possible for me to cope with its greater volume, but there is a temptation to afford less time and attention to the increasing number of people scattered far and wide who claim an interest in my care and prayers. This must be resisted at all costs. I mean that if I fail to resist the temptation to deal with people 'in the mass' and therefore more superficially than otherwise, I not only do a poorer job, but lose my own soul in the sense that I become a shallower person in the course of doing shallower work. I have long held the theory that an individual soul represents a whole world of need, but I am burdened by the necessity increasingly to reckon with this in practice.

The temptation to 'professionalism' is one of the greatest dangers of full-time Christian workers. One sees it not only with oneself, but with others seeking to climb ecclesiastical ladders, and with others who graduate, as they think, to peripatetic or organizational Christian work. I often wonder if such people are aware of the gloss which grows over them as they flit from place to place touching people superficially in the mass, and, ephemerally if at all, as individuals. The perfunctoriness of such service is obvious, even where it is blandly accompanied by a mute appeal to people not to expect them to become too much involved. How can they become involved? They have only so many hours in the day, and so much strength. They are here, there, and everywhere, and cannot do all that is required of them, with a diary full, and correspondence piled high. Yes, but the result is that quality of care is sacrificed for quantity, having to be spread so thinly that at last as far as personal impact is concerned the job is hardly worth doing. Christian butterflies!

I know a minister converted through a well-known evangelist and pastor who was his hero until he went to hear him at a convention. The young man being in the throes of a painful personal problem sought an interview, but since the speaker was an extremely busy man he dealt with his convert in a distressingly perfunctory manner. The truth was that a growing following had turned the dear man into a professional, and attention to his multifarious duties prevented him from devoting the time necessary (assuming he was willing and able to help) to this individual's needs. I reckon that when a man has become so busy that he is not prepared to go to all lengths to meet a legitimate cry for help, he has well-nigh lost himself. At least he has parted company with the ways of his Master. Jesus could handle crowds and, I believe, only went from them when they were too carnally selective of what they wanted from Him. He had always time for individuals in need, and always made them feel that they were worthy of His closest attention, and that other calls, however urgent, even a dying girl, must take their turn.

I am not saying that lesser beings like ourselves are not sometimes faced with delicate decisions when there are seemingly equal calls upon our time and attention. But we must take care to be so divorced from worldly professionalism that we are never preoccupied with the many to the exclusion, or the devaluing, of the individual. The only way to follow Jesus in this is to reckon on His evaluation of the individual soul, as in the story of the ninety-nine and the one sheep lost, or in what He said about the value of a soul outweighing the value of the whole material world (Matt. 16:26).

Nor is this hard to maintain in pastoral work if we are prepared to spend a whole lifetime of Christian service to seek, cherish, nurture, build, and mould for Christ one life that is to last to all eternity. It is simply the way of the world to count heads, and we must not be guilty of it. I think we often are, simply because we have so many to deal with. Then quantity becomes more important than quality, even though history proves that it is often quality at one stage, or in one generation, which produces quantity in the next.

But is busy-ness always the reason for not becoming involved with the individual? I think not. The truth is that we do not like to become too much involved with individuals. Of course we cannot adequately take our Lord's place and approach others as confidently as He, for there is always a reserve to be maintained between fellow-sinners. No man dare know all about another: it is not right, it is not decent. Only God can stand to know all about us and accept us just the same. But we can all come nearer to real, deep, open knowledge of one another with a view to helping, or at least sympathizing—which is often the most healing help we can give.

We can often help others by parting the curtains of mystery that hide ourselves and letting them see that we too are frail creatures subject to common temptations. This gives fellow-sinners in distress confidence to open their hearts to those who, they think, ought to be able to sympathize, and who may be able to help also. Mostly we are afraid to let people know our faults (they see them better than we know, anyway), and because we hold ourselves encased in a façade of unctuousness, they turn away from us, perhaps often suspecting worse than may be the truth.

But it is not only a matter of sharing, which is what fellowship is, or ought to be (it is not fellowship otherwise, whatever else it may be), but the depth of the caring. You see, if we live our lives close to the Lord and some one approaches us, we will hear Him say, 'Now deal with him or her as I would.' Not that Jesus was never sharp with individuals, or that we must never be, even sending someone packing with their faintly-concealed humbug (we must be sure about that, it is so easy to be wrong!). But even a forbidding rejoinder from our Lord was a manifest sign of His care for a person. It was never because He devalued souls that Jesus treated them roughly, but because that was the best way to deal with them—Peter, for example, or Martha.

How much do *you* care? We need to care as Jesus did, setting *His* value on individual souls. What value is that? 'What shall a man give in exchange for his soul?' This drunkard in the gutter, this street woman at the corner, this moronic twirp and that nit-wit of bestiality and thuggery are all souls to whom we are to offer salvation. Most people we have to deal with are not so extreme. They may be far less colourful and not very interesting in themselves. But something makes them tick, and if Jesus was meeting them (is He not, when you meet them?) He certainly would find out what made them 'tick'. This is our job as pastors, even if it takes a lifetime. Do not let us forget for a moment, however clamant the professional and mass needs may be, that *this* is our job. We forget it, I believe, at the peril of our own soul's salvation—I mean its salvation in depth. Our stature in the heavenly scale will depend, I am sure, not so much on how many souls we have won or helped, but on how near to our Lord we have brought them, even if it is only *one* who turns out, in heaven's assessment, to be near enough to His heart to recline, like John, on His bosom.

Let us have a revolution in our sense of values, and eschew mass production, and live for the individual. We may not seem to do much by worldly standards. But we shall at least find our own souls, in depth, as we take time to lead one other soul into the depth of Christ.

Yours both repentantly and hopefully,

WILLIAM STILL

33/SATANIC WILES

October 1972

My Dear Friends,

One thing I have never believed since I received and began to understand the truths of Paul's letter to the Romans is that the forces of good and evil in the Christian soul are equal. One has only to compare fallen Adam with Christ in Romans 5:12–21, and the references to the soul brought to the birth in Christ, over and against inbred sin in Romans 7:17–20 to see that!

Yet it is only recently that, while browsing in the Westminister Confession of Faith, chapter XIII, Of Sanctification, that I saw the full force of the words, 'This sanctification is throughout in the whole man, yet imperfect in this life; since there abide still *some remnants of corruption* in every part: whence arises a continual and irreconcilable war; the flesh lusting against the Spirit, and the Spirit against the flesh. In which war, although the *remaining corruption* for a time may yet prevail; yet through the continual supply of strength from the sanctifying Spirit of Christ, the regenerate part [note the word 'part': we could quibble at it!] doth overcome: and so the saints grow in grace, perfecting holiness in the fear of God.'

We have, of course, in preaching and teaching often led on from this to show that the reason why in this war the 'remaining corruption for a time may yet prevail' is that the dregs of sin which remain are open to stimulation by their author, Satan. Nowhere that we know (apart from Scripture) is this brought out as clearly as in Bunyan's *Pilgrim's Progress*. For example, Christian tells Hopeful of the plight of Little-Faith sleeping where he ought not to have been, in Dead Man's Lane. He was set upon by three sturdy rogues, Faint-heart, Mistrust, and Guilt, who clubbed him and stole his money. Christian then goes on to show that although these three are bad, 'they are but journeymen thieves, and serve under the king of the bottomless pit [the devil], who, if need be, will come in to their aid himself.' Christian goes on to say that he had had the same experience as Little-Faith, and found it a terrible thing that when these three villains (personifying inbred sin) set upon him and he began like a Christian to resist, they gave but a call and in came their master. He, says Christian, is 'at their whistle' and is 'never out of hearing' and 'if at any time they are put to the worst, he comes in to help them.'

For long we have sought to trace the evidence of the working of the enemy of souls in the struggles which the apostle Paul describes in Romans 7. This discernment of the satanic shadow lurking in the background and expressed there in increasingly personal terms until sin is characterized by the word 'evil' itself, has been strongly objected to by those who would otherwise publish what we have written on the subject. But we do not believe we are wrong, nor would we dream of changing what has brought enlightenment and liberation to so many souls. We are not trying to correct Paul, as some have naively thought, by seeking to change his terms, but simply relating this great and vitally practical passage to what the New Testament says elsewhere about the subtlety and personal nature of the forces of evil arrayed against us. One only needs to look at a Concordance to see how often not only Paul but other New Testament witnesses, including our Lord Himself, vary the terms in which the evil we wrestle with is expressed, from sin to

Satan, and Satan to sin. Nor do we believe there is any confusion of the distinction between the terms. But the fact of their double use simply indicates that the New Testament writers saw the one lurking behind the other. Is it not a fact that Satan lies behind sin, and that he is not only the author of it, but constantly stimulates it in the human breast? If this is not true, then we will have to rewrite the New Testament and, contrary to what some seem to think, I will have no part in that.

But the truth is that in intellectual circles in the evangelical church there is acute embarrassment at the discussion of the third dimension of evil, the devil himself. It is time, for the good of this generation, deluded as it is by his satanic impertinence, that we saw this as one of his most cunning tricks. Pooh-pooh the devil and he runs riot, unbeknown to guileless Christians. This is exactly Bunyan's point. Is he wrong?

I was once taken to task at a national conference for having found the devil all through the Old Testament where he is not mentioned, and I answered, Where in the Old Testament, or in the New for that matter, is he not found doing his vile, hidden work as the master of deception and lies? Absolutely nowhere, until he is dealt with finally by our Lord on the Cross. It is interesting, by the way, to note that some admirers of J. S. Stewart have been embarrassed at his later emphasis on the reality of the kingdom of evil.[1]

But the great importance of this to me is not that it enables me to ride a personal hobby-horse, although, as I say, it has liberated many souls who can bear witness to it and who have gone on to teach it with profit to others. It is, rather, to externalise and objectify the struggle between

[1] Cf. Stewart's article, 'On a Neglected Emphasis in New Testament Theology', *Scottish Journal of Theology*, 4 (1951), pp.292–304.

good and evil in the believer, from mere conflict between the new creature and the old remnants of sin within him, to that between the new creature drawing saving power by the Spirit from the indwelling Christ and the remnants of corruption *wrought upon* and *stirred up* with exceeding virulence by the devil himself.

Our struggle, then, since we are new creatures in Christ Jesus and are not on the side of the former man but on that of the new Christian man, is not against ourselves—we *are* new creatures (see Romans 7:17, 20 and 1 John 3:6–10)—but against Satan himself coming in to work hiddenly in the remnant rags of what was formerly our sinful self and deceiving us into thinking that we are getting worse rather than beter and that there is no point whatsoever in trying to be good.

Here is Bunyan again describing Christian's struggles in the Valley of the Shadow of Death: 'I took notice that now poor Christian was so confused, that he did not know his own voice. . . . Just when he was come over against the mouth of the burning pit, one of the wicked ones got behind him, and stepped up softly to him, and, whisperingly, suggested many grievous blasphemies to him, *which he verily thought proceeded from his own mind.* This put Christian more to it than anything that he had met with before; even to think that he should blaspheme him that he loved so much before; yet if he could have helped it, he would not have done it; but he had not the discretion either to stop his ears, or to know from whence came these blasphemies.'

In view of this clear reference to Satan and his demons having access to and attempting to work their wily will upon Christians, I want to call those who read this to witness that those who refuse what has been taught for years unto the liberation of souls, and is amply supported by the Holy Scriptures rightly understood ('Get thee behind me,

Satan,' said Jesus to His beloved Peter), and also supported by so profound a Puritan saint as John Bunyan, *are wrong*, whoever they are and whatever evangelical influence and authority they may claim.

But there is something far more important than polemic here. It is the fact that to objectify the struggle between good and evil in the life of saints has a most healthy effect upon the whole course of their lives. This is acknowledged even by critics, but they refuse the medicine which produces such health.

This teaching alone deals effectually with all satanic preoccupations with sin, and with the injurious, negative and legal attitudes towards the Christian faith which, even in these professedly enlightened days, abound in the evangelical camp.

This negativeness can be best illustrated by a comparison of John the Baptist and Jesus, and by the characterization of John's message in Matthew 11 and Luke 7 as akin to the games which children play (or, in that instance, would not play) in the market place. John's message is described as an invitation to play at funerals, and that of Jesus as an invitation to play at weddings. John for the purpose of this argument is an Old Testament ascetic, denouncing sin; whereas Jesus does not begin with sin at all, in fact and in practice (cf. His dealing with the woman of Samaria, Zacchaeus, and the woman taken in adultery, etc.), but with love for the sinner. He is therefore prepared to associate with the sinner wherever he or she is found, such as in tax-collectors' houses, Pharisees' houses, and with prostitutes in the street. John in prison failed to appreciate the difference between the two attitudes and even doubted whether he had baptized the right man as Messiah.

The truth is that there is, not only in evangelicalism in general, but in our own associated circles, far too much preoccupation with sin, and far too little declaration of and exemplifying in pastoral work the positive truths of edifying love, with a resultant lack of deep caring for people. We can bore people to death with preoccupation with their sins (it is a different thing when the Holy Spirit convicts them). What they need to know is the love of the Saviour who receives them as they are, and proceeds to love them into life by teaching them to objectify evil as over against themselves and as the real enemy within the camp.

I think I know why there is so much negative ministry and pastoral work and why the wrong kind of fear (1 John 4:18) is so injuriously engendered in many lives. It is that men are not sufficiently aware of how much their ministries are affected by their subjective and ingrained psychological attitudes. Being not fully liberated themselves from Faint-heart, Mistrust, and Guilt (especially the last with all its inferiority-producing elements), they tend from the best motives to lash their people in unwitting attempts to achieve the personal cleansing of their own souls. Thus much of the belabouring of people in private as well as in public is an oblique and often unconscious attempt to rid their own souls of a guilt which might have been erased from mental and emotional consciousness by the Spirit long ago.

It is for this reason also that I think men in their preaching, teaching, and writing can become too preoccupied with the world situation and with the evils of the present day. Some are in a ferment concerning insidious influences in the Kirk and in the land who would have every one as hot and bothered as they are over such things. But that agitated frame of mind is far from being the strong bulwark against the spiritual disintegration of Christ's church in the land that some think it is. Some have given their lives to combat the world's evils and have worn themselves out accomplishing nothing because their eyes were on the wrong thing, namely, evils in men. Turn your eyes upon Christ, and He will soon let you see who your enemy really is, and will help you to bind him and rescue souls from his grip. Mere denunciation and fevered polemic will never effectively combat the ills in the Kirk and in society, although, of course, we admit the validity and necessity of protest. But the consistent building up of Christ's people in their most holy and glorious faith will combat these ills and increase the area in the Kirk, and then in the land, where the fruits of that upbuilding will be seen. But notice, as Paul tells us very pertinently in Galatians 5:5, 6, it will only be by 'a faith which works by love'. Faith has no other working power.

I wish all conservative preachers and teachers would see this. If they did, there would not be so many products of allegedly evangelical ministries roving around seeking for that loving care and understanding which alone solves the problems of Christian life and service. 'He who has ears to hear, let him hear'.

Yours sincerely,
WILLIAM STILL

34/THE SERMON ON THE MOUNT (1)

August 1974

Dear Friends,

Having been much engaged recently with questions of the law and ethics in relation to the gospel, I thought we might give attention to the Sermon on the Mount, and provide a short, practical summary of it. It will be most readily followed with a Bible open at Matthew chapters 5–7.

The original law was given at Sinai in the context of the

covenant of grace to a blood-bought, redeemed people in a passover (paschal) relationship with their God. When we recognize this it is easier to see the Sermon as the New Testament law, laying stress, all the way through, on inward observance from the heart (Jer. 31:33) as opposed to outward observance. Yet even the Old Testament saints observed the Decalogue inwardly by that word of faith which Deuteronomy 30:11–14, and Romans 10:5–10 speak of as being so near to those who believe.

The first sixteen verses of Matthew 5, including the Beatitudes, are themselves a summary of the Sermon. By their fascinating sequence of precepts and promises, they outline the pilgrimage of the believing soul, from a profound sense of need of Christ, to that maturity of Christian experience which leads to fruitful witness and service.

The first two Beatitudes describe the soul's sense of spiritual poverty and sin, whereas the third speaks of that meekness which looks to God as the complete Provider of all things needful (and much more besides, see ch. 6:33). This attitude of utter submission to God is summed up in the fourth Beatitude as hunger and thirst for God, whether in terms of righteousness (Christ is our righteousness, 1 Cor. 1:30), or, using the richer world, salvation (which, again, is Christ), or, stating the Beatitude in plain terms, of hungering and thirsting for Christ (see Jn. 6:35).

The chief ground for our suggesting such a sequence arises from the turn which the fifth Beatitude takes, when, instead of the soul's sense of need, we have the soul's response to satisfaction found in Christ. This leads to true Christian compassion and caring. We like to explain 'Blessed are the pure in heart', as reminding the servant of Christ of the dangers of Christian service drawing him away from his first love of Christ (could this have been what was wrong with the Ephesians in Rev. 2:4?). But true Christian compassion not only maintains its hold on Christ as its first love, but goes out on its peace-making mission, not only in terms of peace between man and man (e.g. Jew and Arab, Greek and Turkish Cypriot, Roman Catholic and Protestant in Ireland), but primarily in terms of peace between God and man. It does so by faithfully presenting man's need of peace with God. This peace is the ground of his eternal acceptance with God, and then the basis of good relationships with his fellow.

But we are now warned that this radical solution of the estrangement of man from God and his fellow meets with bitterest hostility, which ultimately leads to persecution on account of the name of Jesus Christ. Hence we come to the promise to those persecuted for the Name, and the heavenly rewards promised to them. For those who maintain their faithful peace-making mission in face of opposition, there follows the function of acting as that salt which preserves society (or 'the community') from corruption. Here it has to be observed that as salt can irretrievably lose its savour and preservative 'tang', so Christians can by complacency (and even by misusing God-given prosperity) lose the cutting edge of their Christian witness and cease to count, and even be disqualified or dismissed as servants of God in the world (see 1 Cor. 9:27).

If the Christian's witness and service in the world may be seen negatively as salt to preserve society from corruption, his function as light may be seen more positively and evangelistically. Jesus is the light of the world, and in Him we are also the light of the world. He has left us in it to represent Him to the world! Light attracts in the dark, and a city set on a hill cannot be hid.

But a light can be quenched, or dimmed, or simply covered over and hidden as men cover and conceal their Christian light when they are ashamed of Christ and of belonging to Him. We are not to be ashamed of Him, for if we do not deliberately hide Him, He will be seen (this is what we may fear!). For He *is* the Light, and if His light is within us, it must show, if it is not hidden.

We are not to flash our light, for that would draw attention to ourselves, and of ourselves we have nothing to offer to needy humanity in their darkness and death. *Let* your light so shine, says Jesus, that men may see your good works (for the light within us will have its result, if the light is not frustrated). Seeing that our good works flow from the light of Christ within us, men will connect them with the heavenly Father, and their praise will rebound to Him. Thus God's purpose in creating a sense of need in the human heart (Matt. 5:3–6) is fulfilled not only in those who feel it, so that praise returns to God from them, but is also fulfilled in those who see their good works, and themselves glorify God and return their praise to Him. God thereby completes two circles, one through us, back to Him, and another through us and those influenced by our light and good works, back to Him! His glory is the goal of everything.

At verse 17 our Lord proceeds to establish the unity of the Old Testament law with the New Testament law. He did not come to abolish the law and the prophets, but to fulfil them:

(1) in His own Person, by His perfect life, in a perfection which no other man has accomplished: and

(2) in His work by His death, paying the penalty of the broken law perfectly for us who have broken it. Every jot and title of the law as expressed spiritually and ethically (not ceremonially) will be fulfilled eventually in the character of those who receive that law by Christ, and who live it out in Him. This they will accomplish, not by outward righteousness, as the scribes and the Pharisees sought to do, but inwardly by the law written on their hearts by the Spirit

of Christ, the Redeemer.

We must learn that the external requirement of the law is not enough, for it does not indicate the state of the heart. For instance, the sixth commandment was driven inwards to require not only that 'Thou shalt not kill', but that thou shalt not harbour even the beginnings of those hateful thoughts which lead to killing. Hatred and even contempt (as well as slaying) are murder.

Similarly with adultery, the thought is the evil thing, which not only pollutes the thinker's mind, but begins to send out to its victims its evil intent. The plucking out of the right eye and cutting off of the right hand are merely harsh and striking ways of conveying how radically such evils require to be dealt with. They can only be dealt with in the human heart by the work of the Spirit bringing the death and resurrection of Jesus Christ to bear on them.

Further, with regard to divorce, it is not divorce in its own act that Jesus is dealing with (that is a simple, but never easy, matter, when circumstances require it, see 1 Cor. 7:10–16), but re-marriage, when a union formed in God's sight (Gen. 2:24)—and what union is not?—is polluted by the intrusion of a third party: 'whom God has joined together, let not man put asunder.' (Matt. 19:6).

As to swearing, the use of the oath by all except the Almighty Himself (see Heb. 6:13–18), is to be regarded as coercion, seeking to invoke an authority one does not possess, hoping to get it, usually unworthily, on one's side. Hence the third commandment (Ex. 20:7), which the Samaritans, and later on, alas, Israel and Judah themselves used, invoking Jehovah's name when they were giving but lip-service to His worship while they turned to other gods (see Jer. 3:16; 23:33–40). A simple Yes or No ought to be sufficient for the use of men who are honest before God.

The *lex talionis* of vv. 38–42 (cf. Ex. 21.24, Lev. 24:20,

Deut. 19:21) was given to limit retribution to exact justice: 'an eye for an eye'—not one hundred eyes for one eye. For while the principle of exact justice is from God, from God there is also a higher principle which ultimately does not conflict with justice, but rather waits in mercy and grace and stays its execution in the hope that the sinner will repent. Retributive justice is God's last resort (see 2 Pet. 3:8, 9). He would have His children exercise His patience with their fellow-sinners, since retribution is not in their hands at all, except by order of God's holy law (and even that contains 'mercy', see Ex. 20:6; 34:5–7), or by the lawfully constituted officers of the state (Rom. 13:1–5). Indeed the divine mercy goes beyond forbearance, and actively showers love upon the sinner in the most extravagant way—heaping coals of 'fire' upon his head and thus seeking to overcome evil with good, in the hope of amendment. Thus vengeance is left to God (Rom. 12:14–21), hence the 'other cheek', the 'cloak' as well as the 'coat', and the 'second mile', and willingly letting the beggar borrow for his need.

In fact this is how God has won us sinners, not only by promulgating a set of principles in the Decalogue to show us how bad we are in His sight by the fall, but by loving us who were enemies and hostile to Him. He even sacrifices His Son with the express intention of drawing us to Himself—and successfully does so. Therefore, since the good God causes His sun to shine and sends His refreshing rain upon the unjust as well as upon the just, we must learn to follow Him in seeking to overcome evil by good, leaving the final issue of our attempts with him. Even the worst of men love their own flesh and blood, but it takes a love planted in the heart by God to love our enemies. This is what Christ gives us, and by the perfection of that living, personal law He lays upon us the challenge of perfection as He is perfect. This is not unreasonable. We must not seek to pull verse 48 down to such words as 'mature' or 'full-grown', for we would never speak of our 'heavenly Father' as 'mature' or 'full-grown', but *perfect*. He will have us perfect, too. We had better face the standard now, since He will have us attain it, else heaven is barred to us.

And has He not the right to challenge us with His perfect demand, when by His gracious Spirit He offers us the full supply to meet it?

Yours sincerely,
WILLIAM STILL

35/THE SERMON ON THE MOUNT (2)

October 1979

Dear Friends,

In my first letter on the Sermon on the Mount I suggested that perhaps chapter 5:1–16 summarised the whole sermon, and gave a conspectus of the Christian life from its inception to maturity and fruitfulness. Verses 17–20 relate the Old Testament law (Ex. 20; Deut. 5) to the New Testament law, as outward to inward, calling for the indwelling Spirit in the heart to fulfil it (Jer. 31:33). The rest of chapter 5 (vv. 21–48) gives comparative instances of the old and the new, '*You have heard that it was said to the men of old . . . but I say unto you . . .*'

Chapter 6, continuing the comparison of old and new, and outward and inward living, first deals with three instances of external religion, performed to be seen of men. By contrast, to live the good life we must yield to the inner intent of a heart set upon pleasing God. These three instances are: giving alms (vv. 2–4); praying (vv. 5–15, including the Lord's Prayer); and fasting (vv. 16–18). These are not to be done to be seen by men, but to please God and serve Him. In verse 19 the contrast between the outward and inward life is expressed in terms of the heavenly versus the earthly. Treasure is to be laid up in heaven, not on earth: it is of a different sort, and is safer there. With v. 22 single-mindedness (to the heavenly ideal) is stressed in terms of the single eye—the light of the life—preventing a division of loyalty in service (24). The spiritual and integrated life having been set forward over against the earthly and the double life, we see (vv. 25–34) the natural, not as unimportant, but as subjugated to the spiritual which controls all, because God, the Father of all, cares for His creation and His children supremely. He will see to it that their bodily needs are met if they put Him and His Kingdom first. There is therefore no cause for anxiety: we are to live a day at a time; we are in God's good hand.

As chapter 6 opened with believing man's attitude to the world of men in general, and went on to consider his hidden thoughts, so chapter 7 opens with the believer's relationship to his brother, whom he is not to condemn, because he also is vulnerable, being just as imperfect (vv. 1–5). None-theless, he is to discern him, and not cast valuable spiritual treasures before gross and brutish men, who like dogs and swine only trample them into the ground (v. 6). The subject of man's needs is again raised (vv. 7–11); not now in simple terms of trusting our heavenly Father, but in more actively asking Him for what is needful. He knows what we need (6:32) but wants us and loves us to ask Him for our needs to be met. If the human analogy is true that a man loves to give good gifts to his children when they ask, how much more will our perfect heavenly Father give good gifts—even a full and continual supply of His Holy Spirit (Lk. 11:9–13)—to the children whom He loves. The sum, then, of our attitude to our fellows in the sight of God is that we do as we would be done by, because we have a heavenly Father who loves His children and would have them love one another. We are to treat all of them with the respect and loving care they receive from God.

But the crucial test of who is a child of God is applied: he is one who single-mindedly seeks the heavenly goal, by however hard a road, only to prove that even on earth it is the best road, leading to a broadening and deepening of life. For those who still are prone to sinful tendencies, detachment from earthly life is the best way to approach it, to prevent enslavement, and enable us to live a free life of happy service. Whereas, if we plunge into this life determined to extract the very last ounce of earthly juice from it, we shall find that it will grow drier and drier, and the road will grow harder, narrower, more uphill—not to say impossibly crowded. Furthermore, one will meet dangerous types, whose chief danger is that they look so right, because they spend so much time hiding the horrid truth about themselves. The truth is that, inside, they are really devourers of other men's souls. You need to look not at them, but at the product of their lives, which may seem impressive at first, but when examined has nothing really good about it, or that does good. Discernment of lives and their fruit is therefore necessary, without condemning. Condemnation is not our part, for we are all under Another, and dare not try to take God's office from Him. He will charge us with the grossest presumption if we seek to do so.

But even while we need to discern the quality of other human lives, without censoriousness, we must look deeper than words, and beyond mountains of superficial, eye-catching deeds (6:1–18). There will be those who know nothing of our heavenly Father and are simply not known by Him, but who nevertheless make a lot of religious and sociological noise about their good deeds. Thus we must learn to try their spirits (1 Jn. 4:1). The primary test of life is not service, but love, both for man and God. This ought to have at least something of a thorough-going, heart-melting quality about it. Those who love and who really bless others are the Christians whom God owns.

Finally, the true life is a matter of living to please God—'who hears these words of mine and does them'. He who does so, is building a future for himself that will stand not only the storms of life, however suddenly and devastatingly they come, but the fires of the last judgment. For love cannot burn away love, although it burns away all that is not love (1 Cor. 13:7, 8).

Not much wonder that such teaching astonished the crowds; it does so still, and yet contains its own unanswerable authority. Is that why it makes men mad?

36/WOMEN IN THE CHURCH

July 1975

Dear Friends,

In view of the advance of what is colloquially called 'Women's Lib.', in society, in parliament and in the church, and particularly in view of a remark made by the new Archbishop of York that 'there is no theological objection to women in the ministry', I thought it was time that the biblical position should be unfolded once more.

May I first say that I was brought up within a branch of the Christian church in which the equality of women with men was absolute—Eva Booth attained the highest rank, that of General in The Salvation Army. I had no particular objection to this while I was in that denomination (although I did not search the Scriptures as I do now). So perhaps I may be regarded as not unduly bigoted against the leadership of women.

There have been exceptional women, since Bible times, who have assumed leadership naturally, there being no man to equal them. But we do not elevate this fact into a principle. The thing that amazes me about the official attitude of the churches—that there is no theological objection to the leadership of women in the church—is that whatever may be said about 'theology' the *Bible* has some of its profoundest things to say *against* the idea of women's leadership. The fact that women are not *functionally equal* with men (1 Tim. 2:12), although *intrinsically equal,* (Gal. 3:28) is one that goes to the foundations of knowledge of the human species, and springs from differentiation in the Triune God.

Let us begin with the profound statement made by Paul following his express objection to the leadership of women (1 Tim. 2:12). He says, 'For Adam was first formed, then Eve; and Adam was not deceived, but the woman was deceived and became a transgressor'. (See also Gen. 3:16.) Now I know that it is customary for this statement of the apostle to be treated with mild scorn and even levity. But can you imagine the great apostle writing to his young son in the faith with his tongue in his cheek? After all, this first letter to Timothy is one of the most valuable documents we have concerning church order, as all branches of the church agree. Is it conceivable that in the midst of it the apostle would turn aside to poke fun at the presumption of women who, it is surely implied by his statement, had in his day essayed to teach, or had been invited to teach in the church?

What is there in the changing fashions of society, in this or any other day, which can overturn such fundamental subordination of women (created second) and subjection (the first to sin) as are involved in Creation and the Fall?

But, it may be argued, the verse which follows about women being 'saved through childbearing if they abide in faith and love and sanctification and sobriety' (1 Tim. 2:15) suggests the gracious overcoming of the disability. Yes, but surely that refers to the second part of Paul's statement concerning Eve being the first human to sin. Not even grace can overturn the first part dealing with the primacy in creation of the male, with woman as his help-meet. We have never met a sensible married woman who did not regard herself in that light. It is a matter of nature, and of innate human psychology. If nature teaches us anything, it teaches us this.

No woman in the happy partnership of marriage is regarded as a second-class partner; nor does she so regard herself, but deeply appreciates the words Peter wrote about women being 'joint heirs of the grace of life.' (1 Pet. 3:7). That is to say, although a woman on earth is to be regarded as functionally different from man, and in that sense subordinate to him, as to the value and dignity of her immortal soul and her heavenly life with Christ she is absolutely equal with man. In the kingdom of heaven Paul tells us there will be no male and female (Gal. 3:28), and Jesus emphasises that there will be no marriage in heaven (Matt. 22:30). Therefore, this passage by itself in Holy Scripture provides a secure and authoritative basis for putting a distinct difference between men and women in Christian service—as in so many other things.

But there is much more in Scripture on the subject. Indeed its whole tenor supports the distinction, and it would never have been possible for denominations to make authoritative declarations about the equality of women in Christian service had there been due reverence for Holy

Scripture. Yet the most eminent ecclesiastics are sublimely and blandly unaware in asserting such a position that they are confusing things which differ, and in doing so are treating the Word of God (of which they profess to be *ministers*, or *servants*!) in a cavalier fashion which practically makes them traitors to it. If we are to be called 'Fundamentalists', then (saving that we reserve the right to explain in which sense we accept it) we would rather own it, for all its odium in the theological and ecclesiastical camps, than be beguiled into betraying anything as fundamental to the Word as the functional distinction between men and women for the duration of their earthly pilgrimage.

Further, the various statements on headship in the New Testament not only set the Persons of the divine Trinity in due order, but relate man to Christ in his due order, and woman to man also. In 1 Corinthians 11 Paul commends the Corinthians for respecting him in everything, and in maintaining the traditions which he had delivered to them. But he wants to be explicit about this one thing, and in his argument plunges midstream into the sequence on order which leads from the divine Father, through the Son, to man, and thence to woman. 'I want you to understand that the head of every man is Christ' [whether he is a Christian or not, for the ordination of the eternal Son of God to be our (human) Saviour is a fact that every man will be faced with at the judgment seat, see Acts 17:31], 'the head of a woman is her husband, and the head of Christ is God.'

This is elementary and cannot be changed to please the fashions of men and their theology. See also the passage which follows (1 Cor. 11:1–16) although that leads into other controversial areas which were apparently as rife in the apostle's day as now. With regard to headship, see also that of Christ (Eph. 1:22: 4:15; Col. 1:18: 2:19; 1 Cor. 3:23); and that of man over woman (Eph. 5:23).

Much more could be said, not least concerning the fact that Jesus, for all his profound respect for womankind, did not choose a woman to be one of the twelve. But the importance of the scriptural statements cited is surely sufficient to convince those who place themselves in submission to Holy Scripture that the matter is in no doubt, but belongs to the fundamental things of God and man.

It remains to state the practical attitude to this clear scriptural evidence, in view of the almost universal capitulation of the church, like other institutions, to the fashionable fad of women's 'liberation'. The matter is not of such immense importance as to cause us to contemplate schism in any form, distasteful as unscriptural practices in the worship and courts of the church must be to Bible believers. Rather, without undue superiority, we may trust to be enabled to tolerate the situation, being moved by the mildness of God's grace. But this does not permit us to weaken our hold on biblical truth, nor must it dissuade us from making that truth known, when in grace and truth we have seemly opportunity.

Of course we recognize that in the history of the church many have left institutional denominations on this account, and for less than this. But we think here the Holy Spirit, who gave our Lord Himself the grace to suffer the vagaries and foibles of the church in His day and never dissociate Himself from it, even when it crucified Him, and gave the apostle Paul the same attitude to his beloved Jewry (Rom. 9:1–5; 10:1) as long as they tolerated him, and as enabled Luther and Wesley to seek reformation and revival within the church as long as it suffered them, will also give us grace to bear with these departures from biblical orthodoxy. But our faith and hope must be that a better day may dawn when the church, at least a sizeable section of it, may return from vain unbiblical wanderings and submit to the authority of

God in His Word and thereafter see days of revival and renewal.

He that has ears to hear, let him hear.

Yours sincerely,
WILLIAM STILL

37/GENTLENESS

August 1975

Dear Friends,

I want to talk about gentleness, which is not easy for one not temperamentally the gentlest. But that is the point. We do not start from temperament, but from the basic fact that gentleness, along with quietness, is an essential element in the Almighty's nature, and in His way of working. Compare the rising of the sun with the noise of jet planes, or the growth of a great tree with the clamant disarray around a rising skyscraper! Of course, God has His force and noise in the wind and waves, thunder and lightning, the earthquake and tidal wave, but these generally intrude upon more gracious rhythms of nature, or erupt only spasmodically.

'Thy gentleness has made me great' says the Psalmist (2 Sam. 22:36; Ps. 18:35). What a wealth of truth God reveals about himself as the gentle shepherd, who gathers the lambs in His bosom, and invites us to come to Him for rest and refreshment! Even his yoke (as a symbol of toil) is easy and light.

God is gentle with His creation. He sweetly controls the moving spheres in space, and wonderfully governs the holy history of redemption to its appointed ends. You see this control of events in words quoted about our Lord in Matthew 12:15–21:

> 'Behold, my servant whom I have chosen,
> my beloved with whom my soul is
> well pleased.
> I will put my Spirit upon him, and he
> shall proclaim justice to the
> Gentiles.
> He will not wrangle or cry aloud, nor
> will any one hear his voice in the
> streets;
> he will not break a bruised reed or
> quench a smouldering wick,
> till he brings justice to victory;
> and in his name will the Gentiles
> hope.'

His is the victory of gentleness, meekness, self-control—all the kindly fruit of the Spirit which He employs for the accomplishment of His sweet will for His people. 'He adorns the humble with victory' (Ps. 149:4). And being gentle of nature, for all His power, He imparts gentleness and meekness to His children, and they become meek like Him:

> 'Blessed are the meek, for they
> shall inherit the earth.'

This was the meekness towards God and man which Moses showed to disgruntled Israel when he cast himself to the ground and called for the Lord to arbitrate. Moses was the meekest man on earth (Num. 12:3). But Israel trembled exceedingly when Moses prostrated himself thus, for they knew they were then in God's hands.

It is this unassertive spirit, willing to yield up its worldly interests in anything or anyone, of which Paul speaks to the Corinthians (1 Cor. 7:29–32a, 35), when he calls them to detachment from husband, wife, sorrow, joy, buying and selling, every worldly concern whatsoever, in order to 'attend upon the Lord without distraction'. 'If any man hate not father and mother . . .' says our Lord; and we know that it is naught injurious to His creatures that Jesus has in mind, rather, the reverse—we only love properly through Jesus.

Do we say it is impossible? Not so; for the potential resides in the spiritual deposit within the believer which is the death and resurrection of Jesus Christ. 'I can do all things in him who strengthens me.'

But such *detachment of mind and heart* from the world in which we live is also expressed more positively in John 15, as *attachment to the Lord Jesus*: 'As the branch cannot bear fruit of itself, unless it abides in the vine, neither can you unless you abide in me . . . He who abides in me and I in him, he it is that bears much fruit, for apart from me you can do nothing . . . If you abide in me, and my words abide in you, ask whatever you will, and it shall be done for you.'

Nor is the idea of abiding, passive, or the idea of resting, vacuous. The word for 'peace' in Hebrew is *shalom*. Its meaning is much fuller than quiescence: it includes health, welfare and prosperity. Possibly on this account some have read richer meaning into the Greek word for 'rest', such as refreshment. 'Yielding' and 'abiding', although apparently passive, are not without effort, albeit God-given effort, well expressed in the paradox of the writer of Hebrews when he bids us '*strive* to enter into rest'. The enemy of God and man sees to it that it is not easy to rest in the Lord. Yet ample provision is made for dealing even with Satan, and keeping him at bay. The Psalmist says,

'Thou preparest a table before me
in the presence of my enemies;
thou anointest my head with oil,
my cup overflows;'

Surely it is a matter of remaining in such positive communion with Jesus that His virtuous power flows through us, healing and invigorating; and from us, speaking peace and health and welfare to others.

It is delightful to rest in the Lord. Therefore wait patiently for Him (Psalm 37), and do only those things which He lovingly moves you to do.

Is this a new idea to you to put into practice, or do you distrust it? Can it really be less efficient, active, healthful or fruitful than our own ideas? Surely not!

Yours sweetly,
WILLIAM STILL

38/HAVE YOU GROWN COLD?

January 1976

Dear Friends,

Now that the New Year is with us, it remains for us all to express to one another gratitude for every token of loving regard, and to see such mutual beneficence as the pattern of our continuing life together. It is about this continuing life together that I want to write.

It is amazing how long we can live under the canopy of Christian profession and yet find in the events, or hardening attitudes of our life, that something or someone is putting us off. He, she, or 'it' is, or they are, always entirely to blame! It is never ourselves! And yet, in the last analysis, it turns out that it is the Lord's people and the Lord Himself who get the 'go-by'. Then, as we come later on to middle age and at last into old age, religion, our professed Christian faith, begins with some to be little more than a formality.

It may be that the evil one himself who is expert in deception has rendered us blind to the fact that all our young life of active Christian worship, service and fellowship was itself a bit of a deception. Something other than the Lord in that total way of life was keeping us going—a friendship, an interest, an activity, or a secretly cherished ambition ultimately frustrated. When the power or attraction of that began to fade or fail there was not enough left to enable us to do more than keep up appearances. Then, as little noticed as possible, we slipped away into our particular form of personal oblivion to live a largely selfish life.

I remember being terribly struck by the words of one I had known as an active evangelical student, who, after a few years of married life with a partner not quite in keeping with his earlier profession, said, 'As we go on in life, the material things come to mean more to us'. If ever I heard a sad remark, it was that one. And how opposite to what mortals should feel—especially Christians! Should it not be the other way round? One of the truest remarks is that the only happy old people are Christians. And we understand why.

But there is not only the sadness of mortals, and professing Christians, becoming more enamoured of materialism as they go on. That is the negative side. There is also the fact that in long years of Christian profession, with all that it has entailed of activity and some sort of enjoyment, there was so little, if any, falling in love with Christ. Of course some folk, thus challenged, say that it is not the Lord they fall out with, but His people. But that, I believe, is always untrue. Ultimately—and this is the essence of the Gospel—the

Lord and His people are one.

If you cannot stand heaven because people are to be there whom you simply refuse to like, then you will be away from the Lord as well as from His odious people. No, it does not make sense. If we brushed aside the devil's lies, and let ourselves see the truth staring us in the face, we might come to see that what has happened is that either we never knew Christ Himself personally at all—a dreadful thought, but undoubtedly true in some cases—or else we have become backsliders. Your love for Christ has grown cold, and naturally you must fill your empty heart with something, or someone else. The fact that you choose, altruistically, to fill it with the very best you know (as well as with a great deal that is selfish) does not cloak the fact that you have preferred something else to Jesus to take possession of your life.

I want to tell you, that however sweetly you may slip into cloistered and comfortable old age and then fade away from this life in a reverie of tranquillity, you will experience a rude awakening on the other side. You will either wake up in hell, which I cry fervently to God to prevent, or else you will wake up to face the glory of Christ with downcast eyes (1 Jn. 2:28; Mk. 8:38), you will prove to be barely saved (1 Cor. 3:15), with nothing to show for years of Christian profession but a gradually waning interest in the things of God.

Think of it again—a decreasing interest, not only in the things of God, but in God Himself as you are carried inexorably on towards the great white throne of His judgment seat. It is a terrible thought, enough to stop you in your tracks, and to cause you to make a complete reappraisal of your life. Whatever the cost in rearrangement, including bravely coming to terms with loved ones, friends, not to say pursuits, pleasures and indulgences, you must turn to the Lord and give yourself afresh to Him. You must look for tokens of His present acceptance of you and the beginnings of a new life in Christ, in which people, and things, and all the world are seen in the light of His pure love alone, and are therefore seen in their true perspective and proportion.

I pray this earnestly for some who are obviously growing cold in their faith and devotion to Christ and His church; and I humbly look for signs of repentance, and of new faith and love, and of a new radiant joy on faces that have long been turned away from Him.

Your burdened Minister,
WILLIAM STILL

39/LOYALTY TO THE LOCAL CHURCH

March 1976

Dear Friends,

One of the hardest things I have to do nowadays is to expose our own dear local congregation to criticism before the section of the public who read this letter. Most of them are sympathetic, but nonetheless when I write something even a little critical of our own people there is generally a responsive exclamation from some one, which makes me feel a sense of shame.

But we must be true above all things (although as Paul says we must 'truth it in love', Eph. 4:15), and what I say now is, alas, too true. It concerns faithfulness in attendance when I happen to be absent, or when someone supposedly not so popular or admired or respected is involved in the ministry. Even some who are within such categories and are esteemed and loved may find themselves sometimes the victims of a largely absent following, and the Minister returns to learn of thinning attendances during his absence.

Indeed, some who would consider themselves highly faithful and loyal supporters of the Lord's work among us, and who would deny that they were chiefly supporters of the man, the Minister, apparently absent themselves at least occasionally in this way. I want all of us who are even tempted to do so, and who vary their loyal support even a little according to who is 'on the bridge', to try to see what a despicable thing it is they do, and to see how deeply faulty and unreliable they are in being so disloyal to their own Christian family.

Sometimes candid people say to me, 'You know, Mr Still, if you were not here, this whole fellowship would collapse.' And they mean it as a compliment! Apart from whatever truth there may be in the statement (and I am almost frightened to look at it from that point of view), does it ever occur to them what they are saying? They are saying: 'Dear Mr Still, in the three decades and more that you have been here, as far as those in the home fellowship are concerned, you have built a rickety, ramshackle construction which, if you withheld your hand from it for even a weekend or a Wednesday or Saturday would almost immediately begin to collapse. O Sir, see what a jerry builder you are!' Those of you who say this kind of thing to me will therefore understand that I would sooner you slapped my face.

But what if it is true, or if there is a sufficient modicum of truth in it for aspersions to be cast upon the work? Then I must conclude that I have not built deeply enough; that there has not been that demolition of self, sin and Satan in the hearts of our Gilcomston family to renew them again as a family enjoying and luxuriating in the liberating and self-sacrificing energies of the new life in Christ. And that hurts terribly deeply.

One of the things I have repeatedly sought to do is to set forward the realities of spiritual death and life in Christ as the only working reality. Indeed, the chief criticism I would make of that policy is that often the negative side, the death side, has been stressed unhealthily (an almost unpardonable imbalance), and people have been lacerated without being healed, have been demolished without being built up, have been pruned without being fertilised.

Even so, apparently the job has not been done thoroughly enough, and some of our people are only 'half dead' to self and therefore only half alive to the gracious sacrifices involved in serving others and remaining true to Christ in the midst of His family. To opt out, however busy or however cold the night or however unwell you feel (it is amazing how unwell we can feel when we are not attracted to an outing—I think most of us are pathetically chicken-hearted and infantile here) is one of the meanest, the sleekiest, most underhand, unworthy things to do. When the under-shepherd is away he is depending on you to keep the home fires burning as he addresses himself to the needs of the wider fellowship of the self-same church of Jesus Christ (there is but one!).

I hope any who are even a little guilty of this will see it and admit it at once, and hereafter make up their minds that whatever it cost, they will see to it that their loyal support of the family is called for when the mere human leader of the family is absent. Otherwise you are serving man, and not God; you are serving a sinner like yourself, and not Jesus Christ.

Now in all honesty I have to say a word about myself in this regard, for there are other loyalties than congregational ones, such as regional and national ones, and loyalties to other denominational groups and inter-denominational societies. I must admit that I am not always as loyal to some of these as I ought to be. I am not excusing myself, and humbly confess that I ought to do better and be more loyal in various directions, especially as far as Presbytery work is concerned; but I believe none-the-less that the chief unit in the Christian church, as in society generally, is the local family, and I would quite unblushingly put my first loyalty there. What do you think about that?

Do think, anyway, not only in view of the fact of an ageing Minister, but in view of the quality of Christian devotion which alone can meet the testing times that may lie ahead, or the subtlety of Satan's enticements at any time and in any age or circumstances. Loyalty to Jesus involves you in being strictly loyal to His family irrespective of who the particular under-shepherd happens to be at any point in time.

Unfortunately, I believe that there are people among us who are capable of reading all this and letting it run off them like the proverbial water off the oily duck's back, who simply take what I have written as more words from the man who is committed to produce so many words every month. Well, all I can say is that one day you and I are to stand before another Man of words, and answer Him. You will not be able to ignore Him. Why ignore Him now!

Yours, deeply exercised,
WILLIAM STILL

40/HAS CHRIST'S BRIGHTNESS DIMMED?

August 1976

Dear Friends,

We are always learning. I thought I had learned a good deal about the effects of the Word of God upon people who took it seriously and who sought to model their lives upon its precepts and principles. But as the healthiest body soon deteriorates without the continual nourishment of food, so does the soul.

I think I have been too confident that men acquiring character by the Word of God within a caring fellowship of saints would be wise enough in any circumstances and situations to ensure the continual feeding of their souls. That they set out intending it I have no doubt; but in the course of the years, where there has been no consistent nourishment conveniently available, or some secondary reason is found for not availing themselves of it, the vision necessarily grows dim and the fire burns low. Men become confused about what is primary and secondary, the offence of the Cross in some form or other creates reaction and resistance, and men become querulous, argumentative, adversely critical and even hostile. Thus the cordiality of fellowship diminishes and identification with fully biblical attitudes becomes hesitant, and at last in word, and, more often in deed, the friendship peters out and we hear no more. Another warrior of God who began bravely falls by the wayside and is out of the march, let alone the battle.

It is infinitely sad. I can now look back over more than three decades of seeking to nurture the souls of promising young people. Although some of the earliest are now middle-aged men and women, in their own right professionally and within their own family circle, I still see them as they were when they took a long look at Jesus and promised, some of them very convincingly, and passionately, to follow Him. And now, while many are still active in the Lord's service and proving fruitful for Him, there are those who are comparable to the dry bones that we read of in Ezekiel, chapter thirty-seven.

It may be that some will never allow themselves to take stock of themselves spiritually until their death-beds—I hope they get time—but even if none to whom these words apply should read them, or reading them be actively affected by them, it is still necessary for me to make a strong appeal to all who have sat under the Word and are still within reach, to take thought for their erstwhile encounter with Christ—(leave the rest of us out of it if you wish).

Has His brightness dimmed for you? Have you become somewhat disillusioned with the Christian life? Do you find it too hard to live according to the ideals which once inspired you and enabled you to set your sights on a lifetime of joyful service? Has it all gone sadly wrong? Even God-given and blessed marriage may have lost lustre, and children (if you dare own it) become a bit of a disappointment. Perhaps such success as you have had in your profession or vocation has failed to afford you the satisfaction you feel you need and have a right to expect. You reluctantly come to the conclusion that the Christian life is not all it is claimed to be, not to say that even Christ Himself seems to be something of a let-down!

Well, if I am voicing your private thoughts, or even wordless feelings and it shocks you to have them expressed, what am I to say?

First, this, that although it challenges the work of our earlier years to say so, perhaps the God you found of old with His Christ and His Word and Spirit was too small for real life. That may very well be my fault, although it could be yours, too. But surely your knowledge of God could still have 'grown' if, despite all, you had fed adequately on the necessary food—His Word!

Which leads me to say this: Christians who go out into untrodden paths, especially in other lands, and find themselves in spiritual wildernesses, or who even in propitious circumstances find the incentive to be the best they can be for Christ flagging too easily, ought to learn to feed themselves.

What happens to anyone who is too lazy to feed his body? He fades and dies. The same with souls!

Dear backsliders, what has happened to you? Have we failed to pray for you with sufficient creativity and faith? That may be so, and in that case the burden of guilt and responsibility is largely ours. But have you no responsibility for finding yourselves spiritually dejected and out of the race? Perhaps even now you are frantically and angrily searching for excuses. That is not good! Have the courage to turn to Christ—never mind anyone else—and ask Him to tell you honestly what He thinks of you and your life. Stop running away from Him, and take a look at His Cross. That could be a complex, yet searching, experience. It would involve a look at what we can only call vital death and devastating life, and prove a real shaking up for you. But if you dare, it could turn out to be the most healing experience of your life.

Some of you made your first confession of Christ publicly, dramatically. This will be different. Get alone, on a hillside, or by a quiet stream or lonely beach, or in your private room, and shut out the whole wide world, and look at Him, as you will have to look at Him on the day of judgment, and ask Him to speak to you. He will speak kindly and truly, and you will begin to live again.

But some of you may be saying, 'This does not apply to me. I have gone on, indeed have outstripped my first monitors, and have found a faith more vital than I found at first and so leave dear old Gilcomston a little behind.' You may even try to hint at this and speak patronisingly of us, and hope we will follow your lead. Fair enough! We have in the past decades, if you remember, learned from many traditions, and some of you will recall that you have sometimes wondered and even feared lest the Minister was too much influenced by the experiences and views of others, and have tried to keep him to his God-given task, as you believed it to be. Now, with new experience you wonder if both you and he have been too conservative.

Well, all I would say about that is, that I think the liveliness of faith and life and worship we have attained over many years now has been on the whole a gradually acquired thing, and although there have been crisis points, our quality of life has mostly come by sweat, toil, tears and even a little blood. Is it right, do you think, for some to come along suddenly and say, 'All that you have gained so arduously through the years is ours now, in a moment, in the twinkling of an eye? Just open your heart to Jesus and let Him flow in in power and sweetness, in love and in joy, and you have everything all at once!'

Well, we know how suddenly Jesus healed and helped and gave joy to needy ones, and we know that His power is far from diminished now. Indeed, the world has not begun to see what Jesus can do and will yet do. But is it really all so easily come by? Is there not a great danger of, easy come, easy go; or, easy come, easy change again? Jesus is a Rock, and, the geologists tell us, the rocks were laid down in primeval infernoes. Real joy and real stability take time. And real love, that can be tried within a fraction of its life without changing, takes time, also. I believe we have still something to teach those of our sons and daughters who are humble enough to learn. We are always learning: why not *they*?

Yours sincerely,
WILLIAM STILL

41/TRENDS IN SINGING PRAISE

December 1976

Dear Friends,

I want to write about trends in singing praise to God. There is a tendency for enthusiastic Christians to sing the very words of Scripture rather than hymns and poems, and where this is done with reverence and good taste it cannot be too highly commended. Indeed, the church might not have gone so far astray during last century and this if she had not been influenced by doubtful (and worse than doubtful) doctrine in hymns.

For this occasion, it is the character and quality of the tunes to which scriptural words are sung which is my chief concern.

It is a long time since I first observed that the character of the music we use in Christian worship affects our own character. The fact is that many marriages of Holy Writ with modern music are unequally yoked, some of them crassly so. It is, of course, not easy to fit worthy music to the Word of God. Great musicians, from Palestrina onwards, through the three great B's: Bach, Beethoven and Brahms, not to forget the superlative Mozart, have explored the twelve-tone scale (all the 'black' and 'white' notes within an octave) with every worthy possibility of time, beat and rhythm. So that modern composers have had to resort to new, daring and even shockingly ingenious stratagems of sound and rhythm to produce original and contemporary effects, with results such as you may hear on the Third

Programme any day to your amazement or amusement according to your taste.

Another important factor here is that whereas musical composers of old, like creative artists in other realms, were considerably influenced and often initially inspired by religion in some form or another to produce their works, it is not so now. Music is almost entirely suggested by the ordinary, secular life of the common people. Light music for dancing, or some such entertainment, is the style which almost universally influences modern music, so that one is not at all surprised to find, in what purport to be deeply serious and religious works, startling jazz effects. The wildest of these in melody, harmony and rhythm are now possible, and among them, especially in the field of rhythm, syncopation is rampant.

What is syncopation? Basically the word means 'to cut off' or 'interrupt', and in music this refers to the interruption of the regular flow of the rhythm of the beat. For instance, in a three-beat tune (such as in waltz time) the strongest beat is, naturally, the first, then the second less so, with the third the weakest of all. Just tap out three beats and repeat that several times, then instead of making the first beat the strongest (the down-beat, as conductors call it) make the second beat strongest, and, even more extreme, the third beat, and you will understand the basics of syncopation. You will be able to explore further possibilities of syncopation if you take a four-beat tune and 'feel' the relative strength of the first and third and then (weaker) the second and fourth beats.

Then try a few tricks of syncopation. Perhaps the simplest form of syncopation is that in which the tune begins on the second beat such as in Parry's 'Jerusalem' and Vaughan Williams' 'For all the saints'. But that is practically Victorian, and is considered very sedate nowadays! Much more advanced syncopation is now the rage, in which you get violent interruptions of the regular flow of the rhythm starting and stopping even at half-beats, all over the place. All this is considered 'mod' and 'with it' and is undoubtedly exciting, intriguing and diverting. Too much so, I think! There is a self-consciousness about most of such music which undoubtedly distracts from the words we may be singing, and more so from the Lord to whom we are supposed to be singing them.

Now, I can hear a storm of criticism about to break over my head, and how readily I shall be shouted down as a square (which I am not, being as young in heart as any!). But I don't care: it is true. The dance hall with its exciting and 'arresting' rhythms has invaded and taken over practically all modern forms of singing praise. To marry all that to words of Holy Scripture, often words about our Lord's holy passion and death, however expertly it is done, is, to say the least, incongruous to the reverent mind.

My complaint is not against allying the words of Scripture to modern music as such. But there are so few new tunes that are not riddled with some form of syncopation. This not only blocks the path to a free singing tune, but distracts and diverts the mind from what one is singing about. The whole idea is to divert and intrigue, and that is bound to interrupt one's train of thought and lead it away from the profound meanings of Holy Writ. It is as if one trying to compose a new tune to a set of spiritual or scriptural words says to himself, 'Now this will not be acceptable to the young bloods unless there is some quirk of melody or some fascinating interruption of rhythm here and there'. And I can hear the said young bloods—not to speak of the not-so-young bloods earnestly trying to keep up with them!—rubbing or clapping their hands and saying with all due excitement, 'Yes, of course: that is what we want. Tunes that don't have that are "square" to us!'

Well, I think that to attach so much vapid frivolity to words to Holy Scripture is to drag it in the mud and degrade God's Word. You cannot dress Jesus up like a clown and expect serious people to accept Him. It is irreverent and incongruous. I am all for interesting harmonies, new tunes, and fresh ways of singing praise to our wonderful God and Saviour, but let us stop jazzing up the Word of God as lately we have had it in these so-called Gospel theatre shows.

They say that the theatre show 'Godspell' ran through the words of practically the whole of the Gospel according to Matthew. I went to see that as well as the film 'Jesus Christ Superstar' on the same day in Edinburgh as an exercise in exploration, and I tell you that, if it is true that I sat through a recital of most of Matthew's Gospel, I hardly knew it! The whole thing was tawdry, cheap, frivolous and debasing in the extreme.

Young people, have your fun as much as is good for you; but when it comes to serious things—not sad but glorious, joyful, glad things, yet sober and serious—let your music match them, and let us never be guilty of turning the worship of our divine Lord and Saviour into anything approaching the rabble of the dance hall or music hall. Gladness with dignity!

I believe there must soon be a reaction to all this syncopated triviality. I long for it to begin, and hope that those willing to listen will heed my words and do all in their power to take the influence of dancing and drinking establishments out of our sacred music.

Yours sincerely,

WILLIAM STILL

42/CHILDREN AND THE CHURCH—(4)

July 1977

Dear Friends,

As a congregation we are approaching the third stage of action in implementing the light God affords us concerning bringing up our children. We want them to be not only believers in the Lord Jesus, but His soldiers. I want to thank parents who have graciously co-operated in discussing this in relation to their families. Naturally I was seeking constructive criticism more than commendation, but the results have been both encouraging and comforting.

There is, perhaps, no more sensitive area of family life than that of bringing up children, and the Christian faith adds to the burden. I am therefore deeply grateful for the help I have received in seeking to formulate a biblical and Reformed policy to cover the needs of varied family situations in a fully Christian context.

I said 'third stage': the first, more than a decade ago, concerned the bringing up of children within the covenant of grace, in faith, not fear. We have abundant testimony from believing and co-operating parents—beyond the congregation as well as within it—that God has been pleased to work according to His Word. Children have delightfully responded to the sure knowledge that they are within the covenant and, brought up within the loving discipline of the faith, by parental as well as ministerial exercise of 'prayer, precept, and example', they have blossomed as little Christians. One of the profoundly moving results of this has been the increasing desire of youngsters to respond to our Lord's redeeming love in seeking Communion. Other ministers and parents in associated fellowships have been obliged to consider this, too.

In keeping with this, but later on, a second stage was concerned with the issue of Sunday School versus church attendance. We owed the initial impulse to act to the reminder that Sunday Schools were first an evangelising agency for children beyond the scope of Christian ordinances and teaching; whereas the Christian church and home (irrespective of day school) hopefully provided ample instruction, admonition and nurture for children of Christian parents to grow up in the faith. I have sufficient evidence that where children from, say, the ages of eight to ten—even younger—are brought to church regularly on Sunday mornings and at the appropriate age on Sunday evenings, no difficulty of transition is encountered, as there is when children outgrow Sunday School and then refuse to come to church.

With our children attending church regularly twice a Sunday (and absorbing Christian truth increasingly, however naughtily they deny it!), the next stage is that children growing up in the Christian faith should begin to fulfil the hope enshrined in the baptismal service that they become soldiers of Christ, in the sense of participating in the battle of prayer. It is surely fatal to wait until children are willing to join the Christian fellowship in prayer. When, by the mere passage of time, will they be willing to do so? Never! the devil will see to that, and experience invariably and unchangingly proves that that is a vain hope.

Our next (and natural) commitment, then, is to bring our children into the total environment of the Christian fellowship, so that prayer as well as worship and study becomes second nature (significant phrase!) to them.

Parents who belonged to Children's church long ago still recall the precious, formative influence of that experience upon their characters. Children's church ended, alas, partly because, after the war, other things were found for children to do on Sunday afternoons, and also because three long sessions per Sunday became heavy for the Minister. If children are to be incorporated into the total life of our congregation, more consideration must obviously be given to them in the services, and I agree with this. Some may feel that too much consideration is presently given to young people of older years who are intellectually able for it, but I can honestly say that I do not prepare for any age group, but simply seek to bring the maximum out of the Word for the formation of Christian character in all, to the glory of God. None-the-less, more can be done to interest the younger element, and I mean to try.

In fact a start is made on Sunday mornings when the lesson is generally presented to the little ones in simplified form, and even adults express appreciation of this. This can be done on Sunday evenings also, before younger ones go home. Changes have already begun to be made at the Saturday evening prayer meeting, which can be developed, as parents co-operate, so that we may be all led back to the paths of our fathers and to more Biblical ways. The future of Christ's church, and of subsequent history, may depend on it.

One further, vital point. In discussing the bringing up of children years ago, when senior Sunday School ended in favour of church attendance, I recall that it was suggested that the home ought to play a larger part in the training of the Christian family. Home school on Sunday afternoons was suggested, but that did not get off the ground, partly because Crusader Classes began to flourish, and they combine an evangelistic element with Bible teaching. We are glad that many of our children are Crusaders, and a number of our members teach in these classes; but this does not absolve Minister, Kirk Session, or parents from prime responsibility for the Christian training of the young.

If the Minister seeks to do his part in the church, parents must seek to do theirs in the home. How regular is family worship in your home? Those who set up and maintain the family altar claim that it is more decisive in its influence upon children than church, because family worship brings God into daily life, and youngsters see the relevance of their faith in practical, homely terms. But the full effect of this gracious discipline may not be seen until youngsters leave home, when the character it engenders is put to the test.

I must say I rejoice at the determination of Christian parents not to neglect family worship despite the busy-ness of modern life. Where there's a will, there's a way. If the future of our children depends on such disciplines more than on grades of examination results at school and college, then they are not optional, but essential. I hope you agree.

Thanks to those who have helped me work out these thoughts.

Yours warmly,
WILLIAM STILL

43/WHAT A FULL LIFE IT IS!

September 1978

Dear Friends,

I cannot forbear to remark on the number of visitors who have been with us this summer. We have not had such a full church during July and August for years, and a great deal of the pleasure has been due to the return on holiday of so many of our ain folk—those we call 'exiles'—with their children. Indeed, on Sundays after the services morning and evening it has been a joy to see so many children and young folk milling around, making friends and generally enjoying themselves in the Lord's house.

I cannot express what this means after years of envisaging and striving to turn a Christian congregation into a real family of the Lord's people. Yet you may still hear people say, even among those comparatively sympathetic to our way of life, 'They've nothing for young people.' No; nothing but what apparently attracts and interests young people today who, having been faced with the beauty and glory and challenge of living their lives for Jesus Christ, go on to seek Him increasingly within the manifold contexts of modern life where His relevance is complete and satisfying.

What queer fixations people acquire which make them go against their better judgment and the sight of their eyes to pursue ideas of traditional ways of living, which, as far as church is concerned, have led to the extreme boredom of our modern society with things Christian and ecclesiastical. It must be a subtle work of Satan which makes people run themselves into such ruts that the 'status quo' and 'the proper thing to do' and conventional modes of behaviour lead them to those blinkered journeys down the same old highways where nothing changes—world without end. What a life!

Yet the Lord is constantly inviting us to come out of our sequestered, pampered and sheltered hideouts and look out upon all the interesting things and people around us, and the new ways of doing things which the exciting and vibrant Word of God suggests. Who could ever be dull with such a Book boring into his heart and mind and understanding? A veritable impossibility!

And so, it is with the greatest possible pleasure that, as

summer (such as it has been, we give thanks to God for small mercies as well as great!) . . . as summer begins to pass into autumn, you are invited within the fellowship of the saints to explore ever new possibilities of living together in company with Jesus Christ.

One of the great things, albeit sometimes terrifying, is to follow the daily news from all over the world and interpret it in the light of a life lived in company with the Governor of the universe. We are really afforded through the Word a continuous running commentary from heaven's highest authority on everything significant happening in the continents and islands of the world.

Not that He tells us everything: that would not be good for us (see 2 Cor. 12:7). But we have sufficient know-how about what is going on and where people and nations are heading, to steer all the straighter a course through our earthly pilgrimage. The corners, bends and sudden lurches are from Satan, not from God. But while we keep close to the Lord in all circumstances, He attends to the devil and uses every inconvenience and interruption graciously to humble, refine and sweeten us. Thus He teaches us that patience and loving care for others that mellows our souls and make us fit companions for those in trouble, and helpmeets to those who battle with the fiercer trials and temptations that assail them along life's way.

What a full life it is! Yet when its source and spring is our personal, intimate fellowship with the Lord Himself, in which we confide to Him our deepest thoughts and feelings, our trembling fears and suspicions also, there is bred truly within us a peace that surpasses all understanding. We may ever wonder why, in a world of so much woe, we can be so serene—whether it is *right* to be so composed—until we see that when there's trouble anywhere and we can lend a hand, we are actually so detached from preoccupation with self, that we run to it with alacrity, and are able to give our whole attention to the other's need, seeking to communicate something of our dear Lord's care. Then it is sharing, sharing, sharing all the way, until we run in again to our privacy, to be renewed by Him, and rested, and fitted for fresh, wonderful adventures of fellowship.

But you may be thinking it is easy for someone well-adjusted and healthy and free to talk like that; not so those bowed down with the multifarious cares of a too-complicated personal or family life. Well, I am in touch with so many people who ought to be at their wits-end with physical pain and mental anguish, not to say fear of imminent death, that I think I can testify that it is *in* the throes of life, most of all, that there are possibilities of deepest peace. Why, some of the most restless and unhappy people in the world are retired from life's main responsibilities and have nothing to do but enjoy the evening of their lives. And what do some of them do? Worry, because they have nothing but a few old-age aches and pains to fret about. No: they are not all like that. Some of the most cheerful souls are those who really enjoy their retirement, and spend their time doing the fascinating things they never had time or energy for when life was so rushed. And one of the beautiful things is that some of them find their greatest satisfaction in caring for those who are worse off than themselves and who need a little extra care.

No, no; it is not our troubles that get us down, but ourselves. But we need have no serious trouble with ourselves as settled and satisfied personalities if our lives are *completed* by the inward presence and glowing Spirit of Him who is both the Author and the Completer of our faith, Christ Jesus.

Yours sincerely,

WILLIAM STILL

44/DON'T BE DULL!

September 1979

Dear Friends,

As the number of evangelical ministries increases in the land, the crying need is for depth of impact as well as geographical spread. Quality makes for quantity. True, in the courts of the Church it is votes that tell in decision-making, but in building local congregations of truly Christian people, it is the quality of the ministry that tells.

The Lord does not call men to this specific service totally unsuited to it. If they are not naturally gifted above the ordinary, surely He is pleased to add to them spiritual gifts. One thing is sure, the apostles were at least men of average, or would you say of more than average ability? Whether the one or the other, the full power of the Spirit made them doubly alive and their vitality was astonishing. One thing they never were after Pentecost was pedestrian.

Some men spark and flash and some men glow; while others pour themselves out in a flow of white heat power. Some men's beam reaches far with a brightness that draws and warms and gently transforms others; but whatever his temperament, the Lord's servant ought never to be dull, if he is in health of body and soul.

Why, then, are some men in their spoken and written ministries pronounced 'dull'? One hears of some whose ministries are correct, or cold, formal and perfunctory. That is understandable, if men have merely professional attitudes towards their work; but men regenerated by the Holy Spirit and specifically called to the holy ministry ought to have more than correctness to recommend them when they preach and lead their folk in worship, or write Pastoral Letters.

Of course, if lives have become bogged down with the cares of this world, or are distracted by its pleasures, the brightness will depart and the unction of the Spirit disappear. Then it may be difficult to tell the difference between an unregenerate man trying to serve the Lord wholly in the energy of the flesh and one who truly knows the Lord but has become temporarily estranged from Him.

There are therefore various reasons why a ministry may be dull, but what real excuse can there be, when the Word of God itself, and equally the Lord who gave it, is so exciting? Surely some sort of pall must descend upon the minister of the Word when all he says sounds deadly flat and unprofitable! I am sure that we have all had the experience of being under some form of ministry which so depressed us that we almost wished the things spoken were not true, so dull did they sound! What a terrible indictment of those called to handle 'the most precious thing this world affords' (the words of our Coronation Service about the Bible)!

This is therefore an appeal to brothers called to handle the Word of God (and it includes men called to lead Bible Classes or Study Groups), that if by nature they are prosaic souls and exceedingly matter-of-fact, they ponder the Word deeply before ministering it, and do not come forth until it has made impact, not only upon minds and hearts, but on wills and consciences also, until their whole beings are aglow with its searching and saving truth. Is this too much to ask even in a busy life? Surely it is the minimum for a task so high. Each sermon or study should be preached as if it was the first and last.

Of course if there is sin in the life, even the much-used preacher can be stale, flat, and unprofitable. He knows what to do. The chagrin and shame of coming down from the pulpit or platform having lacked unction and power sends him to his knees, and he will not lightly come again to his task in that unanointed state.

The same applies to written ministry, especially Pastoral Letters. We as a congregation are fortunate to receive a goodly number of Pastoral Letters from other fellowships, and it is our pleasure to hand them on to our people so that as many as possible may know what is going on in the parishes of our land and therefore pray accordingly. Where there is mutual exchange of communications, chains of prayer can run through the land and beyond, and untold blessing result. As we strengthen one another's hands and hearts in the great task of building a strong church of Jesus Christ in our beloved Scotland, ultimately—please God—impact may be made upon the nation. Why not? It has been done before, and is more sorely needed today than ever.

But why do men called to be ministers in our present needy situation seek to isolate themselves from their brothers in the ministry? Do they know what they miss in terms of the Lord's blessing upon their work, not to say their own souls and their family life, by separating themselves from those who are like-minded? I'm sure some of them do not know, so that it seems to concern them when they hear of a praying company here or there upholding them without other prompting than that of the Holy Spirit, or following receipt of indirect news of the needs of particular ministers and parishes.

Some may think others take too much interest in their work; but is it a sin to be interested in what others are doing for Christ, often in hard places? Surely the last thing a man wants (if he sees his sphere of service as mainly within his own parish) is to interfere with others. But a quiet reference in the privacy of a prayer group to the needs of a neighbouring ministry, or that in another part of the country, can surely do nothing but good, and can hardly be objectionable! Is it not in the interests of us all to be diligent in handling the Word of truth correctly (2 Tim. 2:15), so that we may not be ashamed of our workmanship, in God's sight, or man's?

Talking of workmanship, one of the best challenges to the quality of one's work for the Lord can come from genuine constructive interest on the part of others engaged in the same. And what could not be told of the stimulation of fellow-labourers who simply desired the best to come forth from the Lord's servant, and who were prepared to say so with humble zeal? Even the humblest believers can help here, and no man who desires the best for God can afford to ignore the gentlest hints that such may drop in their search for God and for more and better ministry of His Word. It grieves me when I hear of simple, godly souls deploring the dullness of sermons and Pastoral Letters, and I wonder how the most exciting news in the world, spoken or written, can possibly be boring!

Of course we do not know the stress or strain a minister may be labouring under, in his study or in the pulpit. But none of us is immune from trials and testings, and surely even in the most trying circumstances something ought to come forth from the depth and voluminousness of the great Book itself, to capture and quicken and fire souls to take a new and ever deeper interest in the things of God!

May God help us all to live both within that deep restfulness that passes understanding, and also on the very point of the Holy Spirit's sharpness, to probe, penetrate, and push, until those who attend to us are moved to ever greater zeal and devotion.

Yours sincerely,

WILLIAM STILL

45/THE LIBERAL FAILURE

July 1980

Dear Friends,

Our brother Frank Lyall[1] has written a book *Of Presbyters and Kings* on the legal history of the Church of Scotland. The first of its kind for eighty years it makes fascinating reading. It is lucid and scrupulously fair and, typically, drops significant hints in the most beautifully casual way.

One hint the local reviewer picked up is the possibility of another national upheaval over the faith. Almost in the next breath a senior and highly respected churchman made reference locally to the fact that since the liberal church today is producing less, and the conservative church more, the future Church of Scotland may be smaller and more conservative than liberals will like.

There is a contradiction here. If the liberal church is declining—and with a few remarkable (including one or two theatrical) exceptions it seems to be true—and some conservative churches are flourishing, why should that lead to a contraction of the Church? It would certainly lead to a changing Church, and it appears that many today would rather fade away and die than acquiesce in conservative views. So we are tempted to ask, 'Why will ye die? Is there something so obnoxious about conservative evangelicals that you would rather die than entertain conservative beliefs?

What do they believe? Ah! Is it not strange that our

[1] Professor of Public Law in the University of Aberdeen, and Clerk to the Deacons Court in Gilcomston South Church.

alleged beliefs tend to healthier churches with more men and money than most others? Can our beliefs be so wrong when God blesses us so much? Or is it that God blesses us despite our beliefs which are obscurantist and cannot stand up to the light of modern reason and knowledge?

Well, they are the beliefs which have sustained the church for centuries, and we see nothing that man has discovered through the enlightenment of the 18th, 19th or 20th centuries which obliges him to change views that have the warrant of the Scriptures themselves. God does not change, and His Word does not change. Jesus certainly said so in the Sermon on the Mount (Matt. 5:17–20).

What liberals do not take seriously enough is man's ruin by the Fall and therefore the full implications of his redemption in Christ, and the final judgment for those who are out of Christ. In fact Jesus is the chief biblical exponent of the doctrine of hell. And we must admit that in discussion with mixed groups the point at which conservatives part company with liberals is on their stance on universalism—the belief that all will be saved. It does not seem to worry even the best of these men that they are in radical disagreement with Jesus.

The difference between liberals and conservatives is simply that we take the words of the Bible seriously and believe them, and that seems to work! For when the authority of the Word is harnessed to the power of the Holy Spirit through prayer (it is not always in conservative or Reformed circles!) —dare we mention prayer!—the church is quickened, numbers are added, the Christian life of worship, study, prayer and service becomes soberly exciting. Then the young brought up in nominal church or in infidel homes, hearing of the livingness of Christ and the possibilities of His saving power in their lives, exclaim and expostulate, 'Why have I never been told about this living Christ "who not only saves from sin and hell but offers a life of heaven on earth"?

Why, indeed? Is it not this bogey of what men call 'fundamentalism' which literally frightens them from putting God to the test in their congregations and seeing His extraordinary working power? How long will it be before intelligent men see that they have been vastly misled by their liberal monitors, of whatever school?

In earlier days, when we stood virtually alone, it could have been said, and was said, that we were an anachronistic aberration—something odd out of the past—and many churchmen roundly and bitterly scorned us—although not to their profit. Now one or two honest men take an unprejudiced, albeit not an uncritical look at us, when it is no longer possible to dismiss us as an archaic irrelevance. But how long will it take the Kirk generally to see this? Unless the decline in liberalism is as rapid as is predicted, it may take a long time yet—possibly the demise of a whole generation and the rise of a new generation of churchmen who are willing to face a resurgence of biblical and evangelical Christianity such as alone survives in atheistic lands, and will admit, if not respond to and benefit from, the living truth.

That is why some of us are none too pleased at publicity which alerts the church prematurely to what is happening. Give us the opportunity quietly to show more widely and deeply that God is with us. But those who are beginning to express apprehension realize that they might rise too late against something to which they never gave either respect or credence. For if, after preliminary warnings, the church in general does not take heed, it may indeed be too late. Revival may swallow up a whole dithering, dissimulating and half-hearted church. And serve her right!

Yours sincerely,

WILLIAM STILL

46/CHILDREN AND THE CHURCH—(5)

December 1980

Dear Friends,

Some comment has followed discussions on the subject of incorporating children into the total life of the congregation, and I want to say a little more about it, since it is proving to be one of the most significant developments among us for years.

Let me say again that the insights concerning this came initially through the researches of David Searle of Larbert during his ministry at Newhills. David showed that the place for the teaching of the children of Christians was the church and the home. Sunday Schools on the other hand started originally as evangelistic endeavours, to instruct and win children beyond the reach of Christian homes, and were only justified where there was need of evangelism. Albeit, this applies today to most congregations.

This gave me furiously to think, and to re-think, why it was that so many children and young people attending Sunday School during morning worship (few ever coming to the evening service) sheer away from church at the very age when they need it most; and since youngsters tend to mature at progressively younger ages, the church tends to lose them the faster. I then saw that the only way to be sure of incorporating the next generation in the *life* of the church—not on the fringe while flirting with the world and then hiving off to become worldlings—was to begin with the little ones as we would continue, bringing them into the bosom of the Lord's church from a very early age.

I once consulted Douglas Macmillan,[1] one of my most respected minister friends, on this. He assured me that it was not uncommon in his experience in the Free Church for little children and even infants to attend prayer meetings. My reason for seeking guidance was that we had discontinued Sunday Schools for children over the age of seven. We found that, with the co-operation of parents, our children became accustomed to sitting through church services from the age of eight, and therefore were not subjected to the painful transition from Sunday School to church in their teens. Yet, we could not get them to face prayer meetings. Indeed, some had grown to their mid and late teens and still showed no signs of participating in the prayer battle at all, and there was less and less sign that they would be inclined to do so. The excuse that they were too young and could not understand had long since ceased to apply. But they found other excuses, as people do, and wild horses would not drag them to a prayer meeting, which they considered synonymous with the most unutterable boredom. Think of it! The supreme battle for the souls of men—not to say the soul of the church and the nation—an occasion of unmitigated boredom! Obviously there was some crazy, anti-Christian thinking here, and it had to be demolished.

All right: our children had to be brought to prayer at a much earlier age, so that they might begin to see what a thrilling thing it was to seek God in prayer and watch His answers taking place around them and beyond. This is what we have done, and the results thus far exceed our most sanguine hopes. To hear these little ones take part in prayer in their own simple way is a moving and melting experience.

[1] Professor of Church History and Church Principles in the Free Church College, Edinburgh. He was minister of Dee Street Free Church, Aberdeen, 1966–1974; St Vincent Street Free Church, Glasgow 1974–82.

However, everyone does not approve, and in this as in other matters concerning the young, the tussle is often not with children, but with parents. Yet, the Bible is all in favour, since, in the life of Israel it was expected that children would follow in their fathers' footsteps to a 'thousand generations', not fall away in the second generation and go to the devil in the third!

Some will say, of course, that in the past young folk have been put off by being dragged to church; but it depends on how it is done. To be brought up in the arms of grace, with the law and rules and discipline exercised in a loving context, is as different from legalistic ruthlessness as black is from white. We disdain any such unpsychological method and as deeply deplore it as any. But we fear that parents do not spend sufficient time talking with their children to explain why they are asked and expected to do certain things and live somewhat differently from other children. We have become convinced that whether or not it is due to false modern educational views on the psychology of children, the abilities of even little ones are often greatly under-rated. When they are handled with loving care, good humour and patient perseverance, the degree of co-operation that can be achieved is amazing. This the writer has seen from observing wise parents, and teachers, and from experience.

Therefore all stylized objections to the intention to prevail graciously upon our children to become part of the total life of the larger church family must needs be studiously set aside. We have all failed here. I have failed to see soon enough the necessity of inculcating this biblical pattern into the life of our congregation; and I want to repair that as soon, and as much, as I can.

I plead with others, for the sake of the good of the church and nation in days to come, to bring up their children in the Lord, and in the habit of family worship in the home, and in the bosom of the worshipping, studying and praying fellowship in our churches.

Within a generation this could make such a difference to the church and to the life of our nation, that we and the world would marvel at the change. I believe it is the will of God, and having seen it, I, for one, shall fight (especially in prayer) for its wide adoption in the land, and far beyond.

One further word: there are those who argue on the grounds of psychology that what we do is unnatural for children, and especially little children. There are two things to be said about that. First, is God so awe-ful that we need to shelter the sensitive spirits of our young children from Him? Of course we have to take cognisance of the fact that our children are present with us where we are, and are listening, and we must take care not to offend their sensitive minds. But, are they not present with us also in the home, and do we not manage to take care there? Besides, very few of our little children remain to the end of major sessions of prayer. In this connection, it is interesting to observe the wisdom of parents who slowly extend the time the children remain as they grow older and are able to take more. All are free to find their own way of working this out, and we find in practice that there are no real difficulties: where there's a will, there's a way.

The second thing follows from the first, and we have made passing reference to it already. We are finding that the intelligent understanding of children nurtured in holy things frequently astonishes us; nor do we see signs that they are missing anything that belongs to the happy laughter and playfulness of children.

Our children do not live their lives in prayer meetings any more than they do in playgrounds. We believe they are finding a true balance of life, and are growing up as happy, healthy, and poised souls as any we see, and they are with us at the heart of our Christian lives. *That* is the satisfying thing, and all reports from the homes of those who co-operate are that the children are happier, and their homes sweeter and more integrated establishments than could possibly have been imagined.

Yours sincerely,
WILLIAM STILL

47/HOW TO BEGIN A MINISTRY

September 1981

Dear Friends,

The seasonal church is about to put on its skates (or winter boots) again, and get geared-up for its season's fixtures. To one brought up in a denomination which used to do a great deal of its work in the open-air, the concept of a summer season and winter season was never entertained. Indeed the summer was the time for greater not less activity, and certain branches of the church (often given a lead by evangelicals) have been getting round to that for quite some time now, and that is good. It is almost too trite to say that the devil doesn't take a holiday, so why should God's people desist from good work for any reason at all?

One of the things which a loosening hold on the Scriptures has done to the church in general is to demand less and less, and offer more and more, as inducement to a lighter commitment. The church in society, where it has any standing at all, is now much lower in the scale of people's interests, activities, and obligations. The building is now a place for baptisms, weddings, funerals, parades, and sometimes not even that, for there are nice registry rooms now, and all sorts of facilities for those who do not want the embarrassment of being implicated or associated with anything as 'antiquated' as the church of Jesus Christ. We tend therefore to lower our sights and appoint professionals to keep things going and do the donkey work. But that sort of church is dying fast, and a good thing too, in an age as radically destructive as ours. But what is going to take its place? That is the question. Is not Christ's true church indestructible? Happily we hear from time to time—increasingly, in fact—of young men appointed to traditional situations where a few dedicated souls are determined to continue salvaging the remnants of a formerly glorious or at least respectable church. Ours is to pray for them that things may begin to happen there. But what things?

There's a right and a wrong way of tackling every situation. The right way will depend on the place and the people, and will also depend upon the man appointed. But whatever the particulars, one thing must be constant: if a church is to survive—let alone revive—something deep and revolutionary has to be done. This does not mean that the young man enters a church like the proverbial bull in the china shop. (Even so we heard the other day of a young bullock which entered a house and moved things round a bit, but was soon coaxed out, without too much disaster. This happens to more than bullocks!)

The deep thing that has to be done is to lead the church back to her foundations, for a new up-building. Where there are still remnants of her former pattern of activity, one can begin to work upon these, and quietly but intensively feed the radical Word of God into them, and wait—yes, wait—to see the results.

The remarkable thing is that such a basic intention can have varied and unequal results, which is doubtless due, to some extent, to local and personal factors. But the differences are also due to something more serious than these. Some men see clearly what has to be done, and at what cost, and simply balk at it. They take the lower, easier pathway, lest they do despite to the even tenor of the congregation's sweet way. There, the sleep of death continues undisturbed, and the dying nucleus of older people obviously prefers the smell of that sweet death to the stench of dung. But it is dung which makes gardens grow, and it is the potent 'dung' of the death of our Lord Jesus Christ which alone can revive and renew a withering Kirk.

To wound in love, they say, requires maturity. Pity the youngster then, bent on church business, who has no maturity. But is that necessarily so? They also say you cannot put old heads on young shoulders. But it is largely to young men that the wise preachers in the Wisdom books of the Bible address their searching words. How many times in the book of Proverbs does the preacher say, 'My son'? And James, the Lord's natural brother (although he didn't claim that relationship, but the other, more fruitful one, of servant—was he perhaps ashamed at the earlier events of his career as a brother?)... James says, if any man lacks wisdom, let him ask for it, nothing doubting, and he shall have it. This must be particularly sure to a young man of God set in the midst of a situation which of all things calls for spiritual creativity.

So he need not go into a place and make major mistakes. But if he has been convinced (by theoretical reformers-against the wisdom of our own blessed Lord's gracious practice) that he must begin by hitting hard the sinners in that congregation, then he should know the packet of troubles he is letting himself in for. Of course they are sinners, and need to be saved. But if he would take a leaf out of Jesus' book as He dealt with the woman of Samaria, Zacchaeus, and the adulterous woman, etc... See how successful our Lord was with them! There are some who never learn, because they have been schooled in a regime of theological severity which seems to think saving grace is a rod or birch or heavy-ended club to beat people with. No!

But we are not saying that, if we start more graciously, as some of us wish we had done, the desert will suddenly and uniformly blossom like the rose. The gracious approach may only delay the day of reckoning, when the Word of truth gets under the skin of the suavest of hypocrites. But then, if it is done the gracious way, and a virulent hatred is engendered against the preacher and pastor, it should then be clear that it is the Word of God which does the disturbing and not the unwise temerity of a rash new broom sweeping the potential future church out of the house.

By then there should be a nucleus of faithful souls affording comfort and encouragement to the man at the helm, as well as other little 'boats' from afar with people coming, and going with the Word lodged in their hearts, and blessing the Lord and His servant for his faithfulness. No one can have all the fruits. The important thing is to see the fruit that is there, or is beginning to bud and flower, and to look earnestly at that as the ground of encouragement, and also as a means of enduring the ills which come from opposers and discouragers—not to speak of ills arising from one's own follies and aberrations.

Let all pray that faithful men may take heart and refuse to be discouraged.

Yours faithfully,
WILLIAM STILL

48/SOME THINGS WE HAVE LEARNED

October 1981

Dear Friends,

The first thought for this letter was instantly followed by another, that men begin to speak of their work when it is all but finished, or because they are easing off sufficiently to take time to look back. We are to look forward not backwards, Paul tells the Philippians, and us.

I hope it is true that thinking of what has been said and written in the past is not looking back, either wistfully or reproachfully, but forward hopefully to the fruit of it in the future. Is that too sanguine? Not if what has been spoken and written (or the best of it) has been delved out of God's word—there, all the time to be discovered—and that by God's help, fervently acknowledged.

This I believe: and so I am not surprised that, recently, notice has been taken of what the Lord has been saying and causing to be written over the years. I suppose that next to the cost of maintaining a witness to these things, the greatest trial is the tardiness of others in seizing and applying their truths. Indeed, I sometimes wonder if it is possible for men to feed upon them to their own growth and strength, and yet reject them as a means of feeding others.

Of one thing I am sure: when one has seen the effects of the systematic teaching of the Word of God (as far as one has had insight into it) in the lives of all sorts of people, and especially the effects of austere and searching elements in it, the absence of corroboration is quite unable to dissuade one from propagating it with all resolution and hope. I have had to look back as far as John Bunyan, and others of that ilk and age, to find this truth unfolded.

Yet an encouraging sign recently has been the emergence of support from people who have known little or nothing of all this, and who, coming to see its relevance to their lives and having begun to apply it to themselves and others, have embraced it gladly and eagerly and espoused its cause.

Let every man look to the Lord, and search his heart to find whether he has seized the opportunities afforded him for advancement in the things of God. For there are many 'professional' considerations within the Christian world which weigh heavily with men and may turn them from following, heart and soul, the light they have seen. Straight is the gate and narrow is the way.

I believe that in these decades we have had spiritual opportunities which may not have been open to the church for more than a century, so that without fear or favour we ought to seize all that God is pleased to teach us, by any means, and by any man, in the interests of the future of Christ's church, not only in our own little land, but far beyond it.

What sorts of insights am I thinking of? The first is that of the three dimensions of the Cross dealing all-embracingly and progressively with the threefold enemy of man: his sins, his sin, and the author of his sin and sins, the devil. This is not the place to expound it: it has had a good airing over many years and may be read in much that has been written; but everyone aware of the rudiments of the gospel knows about and ought to understand the first dimension of the cross, concerning the removal of sins; and many devout Christians know the second dimension of death to sin, as unfolded in Romans six. But it is the relation of the second dimension to the third, that of Satan, which is so little understood. To it little credence is given.

Even concerning Romans six, complexity and abstruseness of teaching has confused many as to the meaning of death to sin. An application of the truth taught by John and Peter, about the seed of the death and resurrection of Jesus Christ planted in the heart, simplifies greatly the problem of the tension between the finality of that work of grace and its progressiveness.

However, in practice, it is the discerning of the difference between the enfeebled machinations of inbred sin in the soul (called by the Westminster Confession 'remnants of corruption') and the subtle reinforcement of these remains by the hidden pressures of Satan, which causes many to fall down. They fail to discriminate between the down-drag of their own condemned sinfulness and the huge access of secret power added to that sinfulness by the hidden infusion of satanic evil into their temptations. The result is not only a new depth of sinfulness in their lives; but without a knowledge of Satan's wiles, this is attributed to inbred sin only, so that a heavy weight of accusation and guilt is borne by the deceived soul. This becomes increasingly intolerable, and, for shame, belaboured Christians are soon out of the Christian war and disqualified.

All the teaching in the world about Jesus discerning Satan behind Peter (Matt. 16:23), with its infinite possibilities of application, will not convince many preachers and teachers that this is the cause of hosts of defeated lives. They say we are too much preoccupied with Satan. Certainly that is possible. But where we see Satan in the light of our singular devotion to Christ, and as we draw upon the unimaginable resources of the power of His death and resurrection, the devil cannot become an obsession, but is never forgotten. We *watch,* as well as pray!

Thinking of the link between Romans six and John's and

Peter's notion of the seed of God, we note that another link fraught with much help and blessing is that between Romans six and seven, and the warfare passage of Ephesians six.

Another major insight, that flowing from the biblical teaching on God's covenant of grace, has opened up the new, yet ancient and classical concept of Christ's church as a family of families, rather than as an elaborate organisation. Those who believe that the covenant of grace gives parents the right, by faith, to count their children among the people of God, find no difficulty about accepting this teaching and approving it; but putting it into practice in the present general set up of church life in our land is quite a different thing. What opposition to a simple, homely structure!

We certainly see that this is perhaps only possible, and certainly may be better accomplished, by gradual progress rather than by revolution; but it is surely pathetic—apathetic—for anyone called to leadership in Christ's church to give up the struggle because it may be long. True, the younger generation are impatient, which is paradoxical, since they supposedly hope for more time to work out the transition than older men. But all growth takes time. What would you say to the farmer or gardener who was not prepared to wait until his crop grew? He should not be in the business!

These, then, are two major insights from God's Word which are imperative for the church in our day if she is to survive and ultimately make headway, not only as a church, but in the nation, not to say overseas! We hope that all of us in the ministry, 'lay' as well as 'clerical', are prepared humbly to accept them, live by them, teach them and seek to add new insights to them as these elemental truths are applied to a wide variety of situations, each man in faithfulness to his own God-given personality and bent, and none slavishly following a mere lead. Yet it will be more than a pity if men called by God to help save Christ's church in our day, and for tomorrow, spend half their lifetime trying to prove the truth of what they are presently sceptical of, when it needs above all to be lived out and propagated now.

If people take up these writings, tapes, cassettes; if they even come to hear these truths expounded; and see the fruits of them in churches which have become families of families, with a warm welcome for all, then we cannot but be glad and rejoice and look to a brighter future for God's cause in bonnie Scotland, and beyond.

Yours hopefully,
WILLIAM STILL